20 EVENTS

Structures

THAT CHANGED THE WAY THE WORLD LOOKED

DONNA SINGER

RSVP

RAINTREE
STECK-VAUGHN
P U B L I S H E R S
The Steck-Vaughn Company

Austin, Texas

Consultant: Gary Gerstle, Department of History, The Catholic University of America, Washington, D.C.

Developed for Steck-Vaughn Company by Visual Education Corporation, Princeton, New Jersey

Project Director: Jewel Moulthrop
Editor: Michael Gee
Copy Editor: Margaret P. Roeske
Editorial Assistants: Carol Ciaston, Stacy Tibbetts
Photo Research: Martin A. Levick
Production Supervisor: Maureen Ryan Pancza
Proofreading Management: William A. Murray
Word Processing: Cynthia C. Feldner
Interior Design: Maxson Crandall, Lee Grabarczyk
Cover Design: Maxson Crandall
Page Layout: Maxson Crandall, Lisa Evans-Skopas, Christine Osborne

Raintree Steck-Vaughn Publishers staff

Editor: Shirley Shalit
Project Manager: Joyce Spicer

Library of Congress Cataloging-in-Publication Data

Singer, Donna.
    Structures that changed the way the world looked / Donna Singer.
        p.   cm. — (20 Events)
    Includes bibliographical references and index.
    ISBN 0-8114-4937-8
    1. Monuments—Juvenile literature. [1. Monuments.] I. Title. II. Series.
NA200.S54 1995
720—dc20
94–17475
CIP
AC

Printed and bound in the United States

1 2 3 4 5 6 7 8 9 0   VH   99 98 97 96 95 94

Cover: Begun in 1933, construction of the Golden Gate Bridge took four years (background). Today, it is still one of the longest and most spectacular suspension bridges in the world (inset).

Credits and Acknowledgments
Cover photos: San Francisco Public Library (background); Daniel Moulthrop (inset)
Illustrations: Precision Graphics
Maps: Parrot Graphics

4: Farrell Grehan/Photo Researchers; **5:** Joseph Nettis/Photo Researchers; **6:** Greek National Tourist Office; **7:** Greek National Tourist Office (top), Bridgeman/Art Resource (bottom); **8:** Paolo Koch/Photo Researchers; **9:** Visual Education Corporation; **10:** Steve Elmore; **11:** Erich Lessing/Art Resource; **12:** James Fox (top), Mexico Tourist Office (bottom); **13:** Steve Elmore; **14:** George Holton/Photo Researchers; **15:** John Spragens, Jr./Photo Researchers; **16:** © 1989 N. "Bud" Lazarus; **17:** © 1989 N. "Bud" Lazarus (top), © 1989 N. "Bud" Lazarus (bottom); **18:** Art Resource; **19:** Will & Deni McIntyre/Photo Researchers (top), Ronny Jaques/Photo Researchers (bottom); **20:** Rita Nannini; **21:** Ty & Julie Hotchkiss/Photo Researchers; **22:** Adam Woolfitt/Woodfin Camp; **23:** Jalain Francis/Photo Researchers; **24:** Royal Netherlands Embassy; **25:** Kees Van Den Berg/Photo Researchers (top), H. vd Leeden/Netherlands Tourism Office (bottom); **26:** Adam Woolfitt/Woodfin Camp; **27:** Steve Elmore (top), Steve Elmore (bottom); **28:** Indian Government Tourist Office; **29:** Helen Marcus/Photo Researchers (top), Superstock (bottom); **30:** Library of Congress (top), Library of Congress (bottom); **31:** Superstock; **32:** National Park Service (top), National Park Service (bottom); **33:** National Park Service (top), Steve Elmore (bottom); **34:** The Bettmann Archive (top); The Bettmann Archive (bottom); **35:** Steve Elmore; **36:** Fred Mang, Jr./National Park Service; **37:** Bill Belknap/Photo Researchers (top), Richard Frear/National Park Service (bottom); **38:** Peter Stackpole; **39:** Robert E. David/Golden Gate Bridge, Highway and Transportation District; **41:** Morse Diesel (top), Steve Elmore (bottom); **42:** London Pictures Service

Contents

The Great Pyramid

One of the wonders
of the world,
this monument has
stood for centuries
as a symbol of ancient
Egypt's greatness.

Ancient Egypt

Ancient Egyptians believed that human beings had two separate existences: as a body and as a spirit. After a person died, his or her spirit lived on in the spirit world but returned to the body for food and rest. Therefore, as the spirit's home, the body had to be preserved after death.

Before 3100 B.C., the Egyptians buried their dead in shallow graves in the desert. There the arid environment acted as a preservative.

Eventually, the ancient Egyptians buried their dead in deeper graves, under mounds of sunbaked bricks and rubble. Finally, they built more lasting flat-topped stone structures called *mastabas*.

Mummification The Egyptians had developed a preservation process called mummification. This process involved removing the major organs, such as the brain and heart, and preserving them in huge clay jars. The body was then treated with special salts and tightly wrapped in bandages. The mummy was placed in a tomb along with the clay jars, clothing, food, and other items that the spirit might need.

Pyramid Age Around 2800 B.C., Egyptian royalty became closely associated with the sun. At the same time, their tombs became pyramid-shaped—like a sunbeam—so that the dead monarch could reach the sky and join (or become) the sun god, Re.

During the Third Dynasty, which began in 2686 B.C., the world's first pyramid—called the Step Pyramid—was built at Saqqara. By the beginning of the Fourth Dynasty, smooth-sided pyramids were being built.

▶ This closeup view shows the size and the complicated structure of the pyramid. It is amazing to consider that it was built without iron tools.

Cheops's Spirit Palace

Between 2590 and 2570 B.C., the Great Pyramid was built. Located near the Nile River at Giza, outside modern Cairo, is the tomb of Khufu. (He is known today by the Greek form of his name, Cheops.) One of the world's largest stone structures, Cheops's pyramid has lasted for more than 46 centuries. It was built by thousands of workers equipped with only copper axes, chisels, and saws. They had no iron tools or machines.

Building the Stone Sunburst The stone was quarried from cliffs upriver. Holes were chiseled into the sandstone cliffs, then wooden wedges were hammered into the holes. The wedges were soaked with water, which caused them to swell and split the rock. The blocks of stone were then raised by levers onto huge wooden sleds and transported to the river. About 100 men pulled the sled while 10 men ran alongside to grease the runners beneath the sled. Then the blocks were floated on rafts down the Nile to the building site. From there, each block was dragged up a sloping mud-brick ramp, by 200 or more men, and fitted into place. The pyramid was built from the center outward.

The pyramid is composed of 2.3 million blocks of stone, some weighing as much as 15 tons. It was originally about 481 feet high, but the top 31 feet are missing today. The top tapered to a gold-plated 4-inch-wide capstone. The base of the pyramid covers more than 13 acres. By using the stars in the northern sky, the

Cheops's pyramid was one of many burial structures in the City of the Dead, which included tombs, temples, and smaller pyramids.

builders were able to orient the four faces of the pyramid toward the north, south, east, and west.

The Burial Chamber The pyramid is solid stone except for some internal passageways, an abandoned room called the Queen's Chamber, the magnificent Grand Gallery, and the king's burial chamber. The Grand Gallery is one of the most remarkable achievements of ancient Egypt. It is a long ascending corridor that leads to a passage ending in the king's chamber. The chamber was constructed of polished pink granite. It rises to a delicately carved ceiling of intersecting arches about 28 feet above the floor. A remarkable engineering achievement for the time was the creation of five rooms above its ceiling. The purpose of these rooms was to relieve the weight of the stones above to keep the burial chamber from collapsing.

City of the Dead Cheops's pyramid is part of a group of structures, which together are known as the City of the Dead. Cheops's monument is surrounded by smaller pyramids for his queens and by temples, causeways, and stone mastabas. The mastabas were for the royal family and for the nobles who were to serve the king in the afterlife.

House of Eternity

When Cheops died, his body was brought by barge down the Nile and carried through the Grand Gallery into the burial chamber. The body was placed into an elaborately carved sarcophagus (a stone coffin) and surrounded by everything his spirit would need. The chamber doorway was plugged, and a curse was placed on anyone who might try to enter. The passageways were filled with rubble, and the outer entrance was hidden.

The pharaohs who followed Cheops built more elaborate pyramids, which were filled with tomb paintings and written texts. Near Cheops's temple are the pyramid tombs of his son Chephren and grandson Mycerinus. Chephren also had the famous Sphinx sculpted from a stone outcrop. Before the Pyramid Age ended in 2160 B.C., the pharaohs had built about 80 pyramids. Later dynasties preferred more secure tombs for their afterlife. They built the cave tombs in the Valley of the Kings and Queens at Luxor.

Robbers, Scholars, Tourists The Romans conquered Egypt in 30 B.C. They admired the technical skill of the pyramid builders and left the tombs as they were. When the Arabs conquered Egypt in A.D. 640, however, they looted the pyramids for treasure and stone for building.

Following Napoleon Bonaparte's invasion of Egypt in 1798, the first scholars arrived to study the pyramids. The discovery of the Rosetta stone at this time launched a whole new field of study called Egyptology. The Rosetta stone is a fragment of rock that is covered with a message in three languages—Egyptian hieroglyphics, the spoken Egyptian language of the time, and Greek. The Greek portion provided scholars with the key to deciphering ancient Egyptian languages.

Today, the Egyptian government is working to restore the Giza pyramids and to protect them from the damaging effects of pollution. By doing so, the glory that was ancient Egypt will be preserved for future generations.

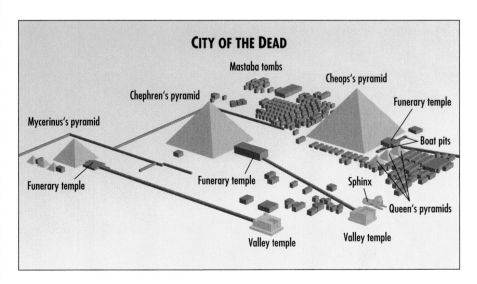

Constructing the buildings and causeways that make up the City of the Dead took vast numbers of workers and great skill. Some of the granite slabs that were used weighed over 30 tons and came from Aswan—a distance of 600 miles.

The Parthenon

As the symbol of ancient
Greek intellectual and
artistic creativity,
the Parthenon
greatly influenced
Western civilization.

Ancient Greece

Ancient Greece consisted of several independent city-states, each with its own government. In 507 B.C., Athens became a democracy and soon emerged as the dominant city-state. The city-states united to defeat the invading Persians at the Battle of Marathon in 490 B.C. In gratitude for their victory, Athenians wanted to honor the goddess Athena Parthenos, the guardian of the city. They began building the Parthenon, dedicated to Athena, the warrior maiden. The Persians returned in 480 B.C., destroying the Parthenon and sacking the city. At the Battle of Salamis in 479 B.C., the Persians finally were defeated.

Greek Temples The Greeks built beautiful temples as homes for their gods and goddesses. These monuments demonstrated the wealth, civic pride, and creative skill of the citizens of each city-state. The early temples were simple one-room halls containing a statue of the deity. By the 5th century B.C., the temples had become more elaborate.

Age of Pericles Many of ancient Greece's most important achievements in the arts, philosophy, government, and mathematics occurred between 477 and 431 B.C.—a period referred to as the Golden Age. For most of that time, Pericles headed the government of Athens. As head of state, Pericles embarked on a major building program to affirm the greatness of Athens and to provide work for the thousands of people left unemployed after the Persian Wars ended.

Athena's Great Temple

The first part of Pericles's plan was to rebuild the Acropolis, which means "the high city." The Acropolis was a sacred place atop a hill in the center of Athens and the site of an ancient fortress. Several structures were built on the Acropolis, the most important of which was the Parthenon.

Built between 447 and 432 B.C., the Parthenon is famous for its emphasis on balance, proportion, and simplicity. It also represents the values that the Greeks considered most important, such as order, justice, beauty, and perfection. Greek architects Ictinus and Callicrates designed the temple. The sculptor Phidias designed the huge ivory and gold statue of Athena that stood inside.

Construction The Parthenon is very large—about 237 feet long and 110 feet wide. The building is about 60 feet high. Its graceful and harmonious appearance is the result of its carefully calculated proportions. The architects based their design on a mathematical pattern. For example, the ratio of the temple's height to its width is the same as the ratio of its length to its width.

At the center of the Parthenon is an enclosed space, called a *cella*. It was divided into two rooms. One room contained the treasury of Athens, and the other contained the statue of Athena. The cella is surrounded by 46 columns. Over the doorway at each end are triangular pediments, or ornamental sections. At one time, sculptures filled the pediments. The eastern pediment

The Parthenon—a temple built to honor the goddess Athena—was constructed atop the Acropolis, a sacred hill overlooking the city of Athens.

depicted scenes of the birth of Athena. The western one showed Athena and Poseidon, god of the sea, fighting for control of Athens.

More than 22,000 tons of marble were transported from Mount Pendelikon, 11 miles from Athens, to the construction site. The blocks were placed on sleds and maneuvered down the mountainside. Then they were drawn across the plain by teams of oxen.

Each column was made of eight to ten sections of marble. Using a system of ramps, pulleys, ropes, and cranes, the marble sections were lifted into place. They were fitted—without mortar—and were held together with metal bars.

Decoration Many colorful sculptures enhanced the exterior of the temple. A continuous sculpted band called a frieze adorned the outer wall of the cella. The frieze showed officials, priests, and ordinary men and women celebrating Athena's birthday. On the outer wall above the columns, a series of small sculpted panels called metopes illustrated scenes of mythological battles.

This segment from the north frieze, showing a procession of horsemen, is part of the collection of Elgin Marbles at the British Museum.

Today, the Greek government continues its efforts to restore and preserve what remains of this great temple.

The Parthenon in History

The Parthenon was dedicated during the annual commemoration of Athena's birth in 438 B.C. The magnificent temple, which could be seen for miles around, proclaimed the greatness of Athens—the center of the civilized world.

By the 3rd century B.C., however, Athens was in decline. The Acropolis was no longer the heart of the city-state, and the Parthenon was no longer a symbol of its glory. In 146 B.C., Greece became a Roman province. The country remained under Roman domination until A.D. 395.

For the next thousand years, Greece was under the political influence of the Byzantine Empire. In 1453, Turkey invaded Greece and controlled that country until 1829. During this period, the Parthenon was used as a Christian church, a Muslim mosque, and a harem.

The Elgin Marbles During the 18th and 19th centuries, wealthy Europeans visited Greece as part of the then-fashionable Grand Tour. This tour was a holiday spent studying art and fine buildings. Many tourists were shocked by the decaying condition of the Parthenon. The temple had been ransacked by treasure hunters. The fabulous statue of

Athena was gone. So were the great doors to her shrine—doors decorated with bronze studs, inlaid ivory, and gold.

Some of the tourists wanted to rescue the temple from total ruin. One such man was Lord Elgin, the British ambassador to the Turkish court. He succeeded in persuading the Turkish ruler to allow him to take several Parthenon sculptures to England for safekeeping. In the early 1800s, the sculptures were removed and shipped to England. Called the Elgin Marbles, they are on display in the British Museum.

Greek Independence Although Greece became an independent country in 1829, it was still plagued by internal problems and outside interference. During World War II, German troops occupied Greece. After the war, the Greek government established a program to restore and preserve the Acropolis. Greece also is trying to arrange the return of the Elgin Marbles.

The achievements of ancient Greece have greatly influenced Western civilization. The designs of many buildings—such as the U.S. Capitol and the British Museum—were influenced by the architecture of the Parthenon.

The Great Wall of China

As the longest structure ever built, the Great Wall served as a defensive, geographic, and cultural boundary for centuries.

Ancient China

During the Shang dynasty, from the 16th to the 11th century B.C., China was divided into many tribal states. Each state built short stretches of wall to protect it from rival states and from invasion by nomadic tribes from the north.

The Ch'in Dynasty In 221 B.C., Shih Huang Ti united China by centralizing military power and taking control of water resources. He became the first emperor of the Ch'in dynasty.

One of Shih's first acts as emperor was to build a series of walls across the northern border. In some areas, workers connected existing walls. In other places, they built new walls. This chain of walls accomplished two goals. First, it provided long-term security from invasion. Second, its construction was a way of occupying the peasants who had lost their land during unification.

The Great Wall was built over mountains and through forests. This section is near Beijing.

The Great Wall Rises

The Great Wall was constructed between 221 and 210 B.C. The official length of the wall—from the seacoast at Shanhaiguan in the northeast to Jiayuguan along the southern border of the Gobi desert—is 1,500 miles. However, when its great loops and curves are taken into account, the length actually is about 3,500 miles. These curves are the result of the builders' taking advantage of the natural defensive features of the land, such as mountains, cliffs, and dense forests.

The Chinese name for the wall is Wan-Li Ch'ang Ch'eng, which means the Long Wall of Ten Thousand Li. A li is equal to about one-third of a mile.

Structure The materials used to build the wall varied from region to region. In some places, piles of rubble and pounded earth formed the basic wall structure. In the rocky area of eastern China, workers laid two huge parallel foundation walls of granite blocks. Then they filled the area between the walls with pounded earth. Workers in the western section built an earthen wall, which they covered with a facing of stone or wood. In the north, workers reinforced an earthen wall with densely planted trees.

The height of the wall varies from 20 to 30 feet. The thickness varies from 25 feet at the base to 20 feet at the top. Along the top of the wall was a stone roadway 16 feet wide.

At regular intervals, laborers constructed supply bases and multilevel buildings to house soldiers. Beacon towers, which were used to send signals, were placed about 11 miles apart along the length of the wall. About 25,000 watchtowers were placed at intervals of two bowshots apart, enabling archers to easily defend the entire wall. Every 200 yards or so, there was an archway. The archways led to stairs that went to the top of the wall.

Forced Labor Hundreds of thousands of peasants were forced from their homes and pressed into service as laborers. Prisoners and political foes also were forced to work. The work was difficult and often dangerous.

Building methods depended on the materials used. When stone was used, the workers formed a human chain, passing the stones from hand to hand. To pound the earth down, workers stamped their feet or used heavy tree trunks. Thousands died. According to legend, a worker has died for every stone in the wall. Because many of the bodies were buried beneath the heavier stones, the wall earned a reputation as "the longest cemetery in the world."

The Wall in History

The Great Wall was a successful defensive barrier. Troops summoned by a beacon fire moved quickly onto and along the wall. Furthermore, supplies were transported easily and efficiently along the wall. Perhaps even more important than its defensive use was the wall's effect on the development of Chinese civilization.

The wall was a cultural boundary that separated the Chinese from what they regarded as the "darkness beyond." It influenced Chinese thinking for more than 2,000 years, making the people suspicious of foreigners. China became isolated and a place of mystery to the rest of the world.

During the 5th and 6th centuries A.D., the wall lost some of its strategic importance, and China was divided into rival states again. In 1273, Kublai Khan led the Mongol invasion of China and destroyed some parts of the wall. He became the first foreigner to control the entire country.

The Ming Dynasty The Mongols were driven out of China in 1368. The emperors of the new Ming dynasty dedicated themselves to rebuilding the wall. The restoration and rebuilding continued until the 16th century. The workers built kilns right near the wall to manufacture the bricks and tiles used to rebuild the wall. Many of the towers and gates were decorated with beautiful carvings.

During Ming rule, the wall became an important line of communication and trade within China. It also became a vital link to the outside world. Caravans loaded with goods came and went through the famous Jade Gate—the westernmost fortification of the wall. Traders crossed the desert west of China on the legendary Silk Road. The gate and the road were named for the jade and the silk that the Chinese traded.

The wall was abandoned after the Manchus, from Manchuria, conquered China and established the Ch'ing dynasty in 1644.

Modern China Parts of the wall have been restored by the Communist government, which came to power in 1949. This was done primarily to help spread the belief that the wall symbolizes the people's hard labor and suffering under past rulers.

Most of what remains of the wall now dates from the Ming dynasty. Only the ancient foundations of Shih Huang Ti's original wall remain. One of the best-preserved sections of the Great Wall of China is the 400-mile stretch between Beijing and the sea. Today, tourists from around the world visit the Great Wall and marvel at this structural achievement.

▶ The Great Wall stretched 1,500 miles across central China. In addition to being a military boundary, the wall served as a cultural boundary between the northern and southern regions of the country.

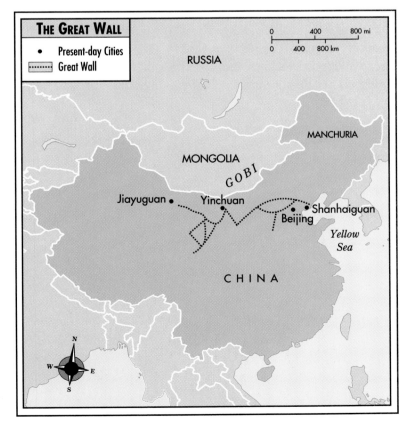

▼ Workers constructed watchtowers for defense (shown here), storage buildings for supplies, and barracks to house soldiers at regular intervals along the length of the wall.

The Colosseum

This famous
amphitheater has
remained for centuries
as a monument
to the engineering and
architectural skill
of ancient Rome.

The Roman World

The Roman Republic was founded in 509 B.C., and Rome became the capital. As the city grew, the state provided for the needs and desires of both the elite and the working poor. The Romans built aqueducts to bring water to the city. They constructed public baths, housing complexes, beautiful fountains, and plazas. Roman leaders also recognized the need to keep the people entertained. As a result, many kinds of festivals and spectacles were held regularly.

In 105 B.C., Rome had its first gladiatorial combat. In these combats, armed men fought each other or fierce animals for the amusement of the spectators. The Romans took the idea of the gladiatorial games from the ancient Etruscans, whom they had conquered. For the Etruscans, these combats were associated with religious rites. The religious significance faded, however, when the Romans adopted the games.

The Roman Empire In 27 B.C., Augustus formed the Roman Empire. The 200-year period of peace that followed is known as the *Pax Romana.* During this golden age, the gladiatorial games grew as each emperor tried to stage a better show than his predecessor. Several years after Rome was destroyed in a fire (A.D. 64), Vespasian, first emperor of the Flavian dynasty, decided to rebuild Rome on a grand scale. A huge amphitheater, or arena, was one of his most ambitious projects.

The Flavian Amphitheater

Construction on the Flavian Amphitheater, later called the Colosseum, began about A.D. 72 and ended in 80, during the reign of Titus. Located near the center of present-day Rome, the Colosseum was the largest outdoor stadium in the region.

Gigantic Arena The Colosseum is oval in shape, measuring 620 feet in length and about 510 feet in width. The four-storied structure is about 157 feet high. The first three stories are composed of a series of arches above columns. Marble busts of famous Romans were placed under the arches. The fourth story, which was added later, has windows and decorative columns, called pilasters, set into the walls. This outer structure surrounds an oval arena. Beneath the arena is a maze of passages and rooms for the gladiators and wild beasts. Elevators operated by ropes and pulleys brought the combatants up to the arena.

The Colosseum held about 45,000 people. A marble terrace, called a podium, provided ringside seats for the emperor and his party. Above the podium was a tier of marble seats, divided into two areas: the first for distinguished citizens, the second for ordinary citizens. A third section was for foreigners. A fourth section, of wooden seats, was for the poor. Brackets attached to poles held an awning in place to protect spectators from rain and sun.

Once a lively center of entertainment for rulers and the masses, the Colosseum has been damaged over the centuries by earthquakes, looters, and pollution. Even in its present state, it still attracts many tourists.

Of the 80 entrances into the amphitheater, two were reserved for the emperor and two for the gladiators. One of the latter entries—the Porta Libitinaria—was small and dark and was used to remove the bodies of slain gladiators. The public entrances and seats were numbered, as they are in modern stadiums.

An Engineering Triumph The Romans were skilled engineers and master builders. They had perfected the arch as both a supportive and a decorative structural element. Arches and columns were the primary elements used in the construction of the Colosseum.

The Romans also used a variety of materials to ensure strength at the bottom of the amphitheater and lightness at the top. Each building material was chosen for its weight-bearing capacity and its own weight.

Local limestone formed the framework of the columns and the arches. Volcanic rock was used for the lower connecting walls. Brick and concrete were used for the upper walls. Lightweight pumice stone formed the curved roof areas. Iron clamps were used to hold the blocks of the walls in place.

The Colosseum was used mainly for gladiatorial combat—sometimes between men, sometimes between men and fierce animals.

COMPARING SPORTS ARENAS					
Arena	**City**	**Completed**	**Primary Sports**	**Capacity**	**Dimensions***
Colosseum	Rome	A.D. 80	Gladiatorial contests	45,000	285 × 180
Rose Bowl	Pasadena	1922	College football	102,000	430 (diameter)
Memorial Coliseum	Los Angeles	1923	Football	92,488	360 × 305
Astrodome	Houston	1965	Baseball Football	55,000 62,000	456 × 288
Hubert H. Humphrey Metrodome	Minneapolis	1982	Baseball Football	56,000 63,000	381 × 360
SkyDome	Toronto	1989	Baseball	50,500	450 × 195

*of playing field (in feet)

Although the Colosseum was built centuries before the stadiums that are listed here, it was not much smaller than modern stadiums.

Rome's Showplace

Titus arranged a spectacular dedication of the Flavian Amphitheater in A.D. 80. Historians estimate that over 500 wild animals and many gladiators were killed during the celebration, which lasted over three months.

The scholar Venerable Bede first called the amphitheater the Colosseum in about A.D. 730. That name supposedly was inspired by the colossal statue of Nero that stood nearby.

Gladiatorial Games Slaves, criminals, and prisoners of war were trained to be gladiators. Each was trained to use a specific weapon: sword and shield, bow and arrow, three-pronged spear, or net. If a gladiator performed well in the arena, he might be given his freedom. If he fought poorly and received the thumbs-down sign from the spectators, he was killed. The day's events lasted from dawn until dusk. To satisfy the Romans' love of spectacle, the arena often was decorated in exotic landscapes. It was even flooded to stage mock sea battles.

Ageless Monument Gladiatorial games were held in the Colosseum until A.D. 404. From then until today, the Colosseum was used only occasionally for public events, such as bullfights, sermons, and concerts. Over the years, the colossal stadium was damaged by earthquakes, and its statues were taken by looters. The Colosseum fell into ruin, and the arena became overgrown with weeds.

During the late Middle Ages, various popes had marble and stone removed from the Colosseum to use in building their monuments and palaces. Restoration of the Colosseum began in the 19th century. Buildings that surrounded the Colosseum were removed, and the arena was cleared. Poets and painters celebrated the Colosseum as a romantic ruin.

Since the late 1940s, it has become a major tourist attraction. Today, the Italian government is trying to preserve the Colosseum from damaging effects of air pollution. Even in its ruined state, the Colosseum remains a symbol of the greatness of ancient Rome.

Palenque

This great temple-city contains some of the finest hieroglyphs and sculptural detail of ancient Mayan civilization.

This is an overview of Palenque, one of the great Mayan city-states.

The Mayan Empire

The golden age of the Mayan civilization lasted from the 3rd to the 10th century A.D. During this time, Mayan city-states covered the present-day countries of Belize and Guatemala and parts of Mexico, Honduras, and El Salvador. Each of these independent city-states had its own government and distinctive artistic style. They were held together by a common religion, culture, and system of writing. This written language was based on about 800 hieroglyphs, pictures or symbols that represented a sound, a syllable, or a word.

Mayan Society A rigid class system structured Mayan society. At the top was the ruler of the city, who was regarded as half man and half god. Next in rank were the nobles, followed by artists and craftspeople. The peasant class was at the bottom. Agricultural and religious festivals dominated daily life. Like many other ancient cultures, the Mayans were concerned with time and the concept of eternity. They developed an accurate calendar and a system of mathematics that included the concept of zero long before that idea was introduced in Europe.

Great Builders Mayans constructed great cities in areas that were covered by swamps, thick forests, and dense jungles. To do so, they had to drain the land, clear the forests, and constantly struggle against the invading jungle. However, the land was rich in building materials, such as limestone, sandstone, volcanic rock, obsidian, and jade. With these materials, the Mayans constructed huge complexes. They built them without the aid of animals or wheeled vehicles. They used rubble and earth for filler and even had a lime mortar to hold layers of stones in place. Workers decorated the buildings with elaborate sculptures, paintings, and stone carvings.

Great Mayan City-States At various times during the centuries of Mayan civilization, individual city-states rose to special prominence. Among the most famous were Tikal (in Guatemala), Copán (in Honduras), and Uxmal, Chichén Itzá, and Palenque (in southeastern Mexico).

Palenque

Located at the edge of a rain forest in the mountains of the present-day Mexican state of Chiapas, Palenque flourished as an important religious center from A.D. 600 to 800. The most outstanding structures were built between 615 and 701, during the reigns of Lord Shield Pacal and his son Chan Bahlum.

The Temple of Inscriptions contains the burial chamber of the Mayan ruler Pacal. Sculptures and carvings tell about his ancestry, his life, and his afterlife.

Temple of Inscriptions Many of the hundreds of structures at Palenque are temple-tombs. The most important of these is the Temple of Inscriptions, so named because of the panels of hieroglyphs adorning the main entrance. It is the largest tomb in Middle America, and it was built for Lord Shield Pacal in A.D. 682.

The base is a stepped pyramid that stands 75 feet high. A temple, located on a platform, is at the pyramid's summit. Stucco figures and carved glyphs in the temple tell the story of Pacal's ancestry, life, death, and divinity. The crypt of Pacal is in a secret chamber located in the central core of the pyramid. It is reached by a steep flight of stairs from the rear gallery's central chamber.

The Palace Complex Built over a period of 120 years, the palace complex is a maze of courtyards, galleries, rooms, and underground passageways. Historians believe that the palace served as a government center rather than as a royal residence. Located in the palace's northeast

Archaeologists have learned much about Mayan history from friezes such as this one. Unfortunately, many have been damaged over time or were looted by explorers in the 18th and 19th centuries.

courtyard are the longest intact Mayan hieroglyphs and several life-size sculptures. The palace complex also has a four-story tower, a feature that is unique to Mayan architecture. The tower was probably used for astronomical observations.

Building Methods The Mayans followed a highly detailed construction plan. Some workers shaped the stones, others roughly sculpted the blocks, and expert masons finished them. Peasants carried small stones and supplies on their backs. Larger stone blocks were moved using a system of log rollers. Craftspeople used simple flint and obsidian tools for polishing and plastering. Artists used jade and flint tools for carving.

The Mystery of Palenque

Palenque's importance as a ceremonial center declined rapidly after A.D. 800. For reasons still unknown, this once-thriving city was abandoned by 820. By the time Spanish conqueror Hernan Cortés invaded the Yucatán in the 1520s, Palenque lay forgotten and hidden by the dense forest. Cortés passed within 30 miles of the city, yet his Indian guide did not even know of its existence.

Rediscovery and Rebirth American explorer John L. Stephens discovered Palenque in the 19th century. Since then, many archaeologists have worked to uncover this ancient city. In 1949, the crypt of Pacal was discovered when an archaeologist was examining the Temple of Inscriptions. As he lifted a floor stone that had concealed handholds, he saw the rubble-filled stairway. The crypt had survived the centuries undisturbed. A jade mask was still covering Pacal's face.

Today, archaeologists are still working on the Palenque site and piecing together its history. A growing number of tourists make their way to the ruins each year. Some of Palenque's greatness can be seen, but many mysteries are still waiting to be unraveled.

The stairway leading to Pacal's burial chamber was deliberately strewn with rubble to prevent anyone from entering the tomb.

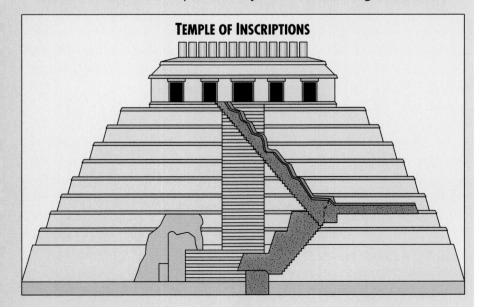

TEMPLE OF INSCRIPTIONS

Angkor

In these ancient Cambodian ruins are some of the world's most impressive Hindu monuments.

The Khmer Empire

In A.D. 802, King Jayavarman united the Khmer people. Their country was then called Kambuja, from which the later names of Cambodia and Kampuchea were derived. In the language of the Khmer, *Angkor* means "the capital." Geographically, Angkor consists

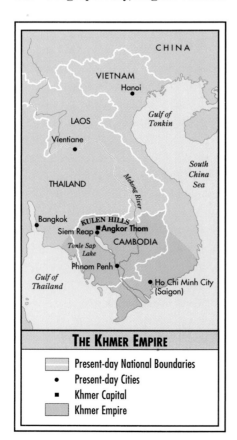

THE KHMER EMPIRE

- Present-day National Boundaries
- • Present-day Cities
- ■ Khmer Capital
- Khmer Empire

of about 75 square miles of fertile plains near Tonle Sap lake. The Khmer Empire flourished between the 9th and the 14th centuries. During that time, the empire extended its power and influence to become the strongest and most advanced civilization in Southeast Asia.

The success of the empire was due in large part to the Khmer's ability to control the water supply. They developed a sophisticated network of canals that made the area fertile for rice farming. The Khmer built huge reservoirs called *baray*. These were used to store water from the monsoons and snow runoff, which was needed during the dry season.

Influenced by the Hindu traders from India, the Khmer adopted their own version of Hinduism around 802. They identified their earthly king with the Hindu gods. This connection became the basis for all social, political, and artistic life. The Khmer kings constructed several capitals, but none was more artistically or technically advanced than the capital city of Angkor.

The ancient Khmer Empire occupied much of the modern countries of Cambodia, Vietnam, and Thailand.

One of the most beautiful temples in the world, Angkor Wat took nearly four decades to construct and extends over an area of nearly one square mile.

The Splendor of Angkor

Centuries after the completion of Angkor's ancient monuments, local residents were asked about the builders. They replied that Angkor was built "by the king of the angels" or "by giants," or that it was "made by itself." Certainly, its splendor suggests superhuman skill.

Angkor was designed as a symbol of the Khmer's religious and political power. The city is arranged around several temples connected by a vast system of human-made waterways and wide highways. The people were required to work for a part of each year of their lives building, repairing, or maintaining the city.

Phnom Bakheng Each Khmer king built his own temple; Yasovarman I was the first major builder of Angkor. In 889, he constructed the great Eastern Baray, the first irrigation project. He diverted the Siem Reap River to fill this great reservoir, which measured four miles long by one mile wide.

On a natural hill, Yasovarman built his temple—Phnom Bakheng.

The first temple at Angkor, Phnom Bakheng consists of 108 tower-shrines built on top of a series of terraced pyramids.

Hindu Temple Angkor Wat is one of the largest and most beautiful temples in the world. It was designed by the king's architect and built by artisans and laborers using a wax model as a plan. Its construction—completed in 1150—took 37 years, as workers transported stones by ox-carts from the surrounding area. Covering nearly a full square mile, the temple reflects the perfect symmetry of classic Khmer architecture and the Hindu view of the universe. It is reached by several causeways over a moat, which symbolizes the mythical ocean from which life sprang. Within the outer wall are several rectangular enclosures and a central tower surrounded by four smaller towers in the form of lotus buds. The central tower represents sacred Mount Meru, the home of the gods and the center of the universe. Built on a pyramid-shaped base more than 200 feet high, the temple is reached by staircases on each of the pyramid's sides.

The outer wall consists of a gallery that is covered with carefully detailed raised sculptures called *bas-reliefs*. These sculptures recount the myths of Hindu gods—Vishnu, Krishna, and Rama—and tales of the royal family. The various sections of the temple are linked by a series of columns lined with elaborate sculptures and immense carvings. Inside are shrines, passageways, staircases, and many statues.

Jayavarman VII In 1177, the Cham people, from what is now Vietnam, invaded Angkor and sacked the city. King Jayavarman VII took his revenge on the Cham and began a frenzy of construction. Believing that the Hindu gods had failed to protect the city, he dedicated the new capital, Angkor Thom, and his temple, Bayon, to Buddha.

Compared to the perfect symmetry of Angkor Wat, Bayon seems cluttered and less well built. A causeway leading to the entrance is lined with 54 giant figures tugging on a sacred serpent. It has clifflike walls and more than 50 towers, with the huge smiling face of Jayavarman carved on each side of the towers. In the end, Jayavarman's extensive building plan sapped the energy of the empire and hastened its decline.

Angkor in Ruins

In 1431, the Khmer abandoned Angkor after Thai forces invaded the city. Angkor was forgotten for 400 years and was overrun by the jungle. The Khmer had used trenches filled with fine sand for the foundations of their temples. Centuries of rain seeping into the foundations caused stones to shift and crack. Rainwater also caused the clay in the sandstone—the chief building material—to dissolve, weakening the structures.

In 1860, the French naturalist Alexandre-Henri Mouhot rediscovered the city while on a wildlife expedition. His enthusiastic reports convinced the French government, which then controlled this region of Southeast Asia, to begin a systematic study of the ruins. In 1898, the French committed substantial funds for the preservation of the monuments at Angkor.

In 1975, the Communist Khmer Rouge captured Cambodia, renaming the country Kampuchea. Three years later, Vietnamese Communists gained control of the country. During the next 13 years of fighting, the monuments at Angkor were further damaged by looters, bullets, and graffiti.

In 1991, a United Nations peacekeeping force took control in Cambodia. Two years later, Cambodia's four main political factions signed a new constitution that restored the monarchy. Prince Norodom Sihanouk became the king of Cambodia. However, the fate of the great temple-city of Angkor is still unknown.

This wall carving at the Bayon shows a scene from an ancient battle.

15

Great Zimbabwe

This ancient fortress in southern Zimbabwe represents a high point of Iron Age civilization in sub-Saharan Africa.

The Bantu Peoples

More than 180 million black Africans, belonging to 300 different tribal groups, make up the Bantu peoples. They originally lived in the area that is now Cameroon. About the time of Christ, a great Bantu migration occurred. The different groups established areas of political power. During the 9th century A.D., one such group—the Karanga—built a power base in what is now Zimbabwe. They built a town 250 miles inland from the coast at the head of the long wide valley of the Mtilikwe River—near the present-day road that links the capital city of Harare and Johannesburg, South Africa.

The town grew rapidly and became a major trading center. At ports on the east coast of Africa, the Karanga traded copper, ivory, and gold for porcelain, cloth, and beads from China, India, and Indonesia.

The Great Stone Houses

Translated from the Bantu language, the word *zimbabwe* means "house of stone." Built during the empire period (950 to 1450), Great Zimbabwe is one of the largest stone monuments in Africa. Great Zimbabwe covers about 60 acres and includes two major structures: the Acropolis and the temple complex.

The Acropolis

This fortresslike series of walls was built on a natural granite outcrop, or rock spur. With remarkable skill, the builders cut granite blocks, which they piled above and along the natural contours of the rocks. Within the walls was a maze of passages, steps, and corridors. These corridors led to seven towers, which probably were used for observation and defense. Only four of the towers remain standing.

AFRICAN KINGDOMS BEFORE 1600

- Present-day Cities

Ancient Zimbabwe Sphere of Influence

Many great kingdoms thrived in early Africa. This map shows some of them.

The Temple

The temple complex was built within a great elliptical enclosure that measured 800 yards long and 70 yards wide. The outer wall was 20 feet thick and ranged in height from 16 to 35 feet. It was made from blue-gray granite, which was cut square and laid like bricks. Interior walls originally divided the area into several distinct enclosures. Each section had a group of mud huts, but only the bases and some walls remain. The temple complex was probably the ruler's residence, and the great outer wall kept his life secret from public view.

For years, archaeologists searched for a way to enter this tower. Its purpose still remains a mystery.

The chevron pattern at the top of this wall remains a mystery. Since the wall has no openings or means of climbing, it may have been a fortress.

The chevron pattern at the top of this wall remains a mystery. Since the wall has no openings or means of climbing, it may have been a fortress.

Construction It is believed that each member of the community participated, for a specified period, in the building of the stone city. They removed stone from outcrops throughout the valley. Some granite blocks were left in their natural rough state, and others were shaped and finished with simple iron tools. The stones were set together without mortar. A mixture of gravel and clay was used to form the round tops of walls. The builders developed a method of placing the stones so that the walls tapered gradually as they rose. This tapering made the tops of walls several feet narrower than the lower sections. This technique also made the walls more self-supporting.

Special Features There are several features of special interest at Great Zimbabwe.

- Eight pillars topped by sculpted soapstone birds are thought to be monuments honoring dead rulers.
- A fairly sophisticated drainage system was built into the outer wall.
- A mysterious chevron pattern of inverted V shapes was worked into the top portion of the southern wall.
- A mysterious conical tower, which has no opening and no easy way to climb it, was built.

In 1929, archaeologists excavated beneath this 30-foot cone-shaped structure. They learned little from their exploration, and the original purpose of the tower is still a mystery.

The Twilight of Zimbabwe

In the late 1400s, the Rozwi—a rebellious group in the south—took over the city of Zimbabwe and established the Changamire Empire. In the 16th century, the Portuguese colonized the coastal areas of eastern Africa. They traded with the natives in parts of the interior but never reached the great stone city.

By the late 1700s, the empire was in decline. Weakened by fights for the throne and threatened by the growing power of other Bantu groups—most notably the Zulu nation—the remaining people were driven from Great Zimbabwe during the 1830s.

The Mystery of Zimbabwe In the 1870s, German geologist Karl Mauch became the first European to see the ruins of Great Zimbabwe. He thought that he had found the location of either the biblical king Solomon's gold mines or the legendary kingdom of Prester John (the priest who ruled a Christian kingdom in Asia or Africa in the Middle Ages). Mauch's published report of his findings intrigued others, and a steady stream of Europeans arrived in the area. A few came in the hope of unraveling the mystery of Great Zimbabwe. But most came as treasure seekers.

Unfortunately, the treasure seekers were careless about their excavations and felt no need to keep accurate records of their findings. As a result, serious scholars had difficulty identifying Zimbabwe's builders. For a time, some scholars speculated that the city had been built by ancient peoples of the East, perhaps from Arabia.

In the 1940s and 1950s, carefully planned archaeological studies were made of the Zimbabwe ruins. The results indicated that Great Zimbabwe was built by native Africans, ancestors of the Mashona people who live in the country today. Although much still is unknown about the ancient stone city, Great Zimbabwe is recognized as one of the world's great structural achievements.

Archaeologists discovered eight carved birds perched on pillars. They believe that these birds may have been monuments to dead chiefs and ancestors.

The Tower of London

A symbol of royal power, this famous monument recalls nine centuries of British history.

A panel from the Bayeux tapestry shows the Battle of Hastings, which was won by William the Conquerer in 1066.

Anglo-Saxon England

England was a dangerous place to live during the Anglo-Saxon period from 449 to 1066. It was a time of violence, chaos, and warfare. The country was divided into several warring kingdoms. During the 8th century, these kingdoms united in order to resist Viking invasions. For protection against those invaders, people lived in walled towns, going outside only to till the land. Noblemen built an early type of castle fortification called a *motte and bailey*. It was an enclosed wooden construction situated on a mound and surrounded by a ditch. However, advances in weaponry and combat tactics made such castles increasingly vulnerable to attack.

Norman Conquest When King Edward the Confessor died in 1066, rival claims to the English throne were made by Harold (last of the Saxon kings) and William (the Duke of Normandy in France). William, nicknamed "the Conqueror," invaded England and defeated Harold at the Battle of Hastings on October 15, 1066. He was crowned king of England on Christmas Day.

Building a Fortress

One of William's first acts as king was to construct a series of castles in southeastern England. The most important of these castles was located along the Thames River in London, the largest and most powerful of England's walled cities. The first structure in the London complex was the *keep,* completed in 1098. A keep is the strongest and most secure tower, usually located in the middle of a castle. The Tower of London keep was one of the first such structures to be made of stone. The walls vary in thickness from 15 feet at the base to 11 feet at the top. Called the White Tower, the keep dominates the castle complex. Its only entrance was reached by a removable wooden staircase. Inside were the king's apartment and private chapel, large storage areas, and living quarters for the constable who administered Tower affairs. During the 12th century, other parts of the Tower complex were built, including:

- a chapel for Tower residents;
- the Wardrobe Tower for the monarch's clothes, armor, treasury, and jewels;
- the unique round Bell Tower; and
- extensions to defensive walls.

The Tower complex was further expanded during the reigns of Henry III and his son, Edward I. By 1307, it had taken the shape it has today. Henry III, an expert in castle construction, built a ring of 11 towers and battlements around the White Tower. He also surrounded the entire structure with a moat 20 feet deep. Each tower had its own design and purpose, although all were used as prisons. The Wakefield Tower served as a royal residence for most of the medieval period, from 1066 to 1485, and it became notorious as the place where King Henry VI was murdered in 1471. The Salt Tower, originally used for storage, is remembered as the prison where priests were tortured during the 1500s.

Edward I, who reigned from 1272 to 1307, transformed the Tower into a fortress consisting of two defensive walls circling the White Tower. He also built the Middle Tower, which is the main visitors' entrance today. He added a water entrance that came to be known as Traitors' Gate. It was through this gate that political prisoners were brought by boat for imprisonment in the tower. Because of its strong fortifications, the Tower of London became the primary castle whenever the king needed a refuge.

Originally built as a fortress, the Tower of London has served as a royal residence, a prison, an arsenal, and a safety vault for the crown jewels.

The World of the Tower

The Tower served as a royal residence and fortress until 1547. It also has served other functions, such as:

- the Royal Mint until 1807;
- the main public records office until the mid-1800s;
- the national arsenal and military administration center until the late 1800s;
- the safe for the crown jewels since 1303; and
- the Royal Menagerie from 1235, when Henry III received some animals as gifts, until the 1800s when they were moved to a zoo.

Bloody History Much of the modern fascination with the Tower comes from its reputation as a prison and the scene of many gruesome murders and executions. Only nobility were imprisoned and executed in the Tower. Commoners were executed on nearby Tower Hill, and their heads were displayed on the spikes of London Bridge.

King Edward IV reportedly had his brother executed by drowning him in a wine cask in the Tower. King Richard III, according to legend, had his young nephews murdered here.

Henry VIII used the Tower as a prison and execution stage for those who angered him. Two of Henry's wives, Anne Boleyn and Catherine Howard, were beheaded in the Tower. The Tower was last used as a prison during World War II, and the last execution held there—of a German spy—was in 1941.

Tourist Attraction During the 18th century, the Tower ceased to be a center for national government, and several of the buildings were opened for public viewing. The Tower became a major tourist attraction during the 19th century, when the menagerie, mint, and state records were moved elsewhere. Buildings were restored, and the moat was filled and planted with grass. Today, over two million tourists a year visit the Tower and walk the battlements. The Yeoman Warders, called Beefeaters for their rugged appearance, once guarded the Tower complex.

Today, they entertain tourists with their stories of the ghosts and ravens that inhabit the Tower. According to legend, the British monarchy will fall when the ravens leave the Tower of London.

Tourists enjoy listening to the Yeoman Warders, who recount the history and legends of the Tower.

Anasazi Cliff Dwellings

More than
a thousand years ago,
the Anasazi built
"apartment complexes"
in cliff caves.

Ancient Americans

The Anasazi were a tribe of hunter-gatherers and the ancestors of to-day's Pueblo people of the American Southwest. Although much of their history is still a mystery, researchers know that around 3000 B.C. they migrated north from what is now southern New Mexico. The probable reason for this move was to find food for an increasing population.

The Anasazi settled in the area that is known today as the Four Corners. It is where four states—Arizona, New Mexico, Colorado, and Utah—meet. This region is famous for its deep canyons and high tablelands. The latter consist of wide plateaus and steep-sided mesas rising from the canyon floors.

By A.D. 500, the Anasazi had become farmers, growing corn and other crops in the fertile canyon bottoms. Sheltered by the mesa cliffs, they built permanent multiple-family settlements. Most of these were pit houses—shallow pits covered by roofs made of thatch and mud and held up by poles.

Much of what we know about these Native Americans comes from studying their pottery and rock art. In addition to their elaborately decorated pottery, the Anasazi carved rock pictures, called *petroglyphs,* into the canyon walls.

Rise of the Pueblos Between 750 and 1100, the Anasazi established villages of multistoried buildings called *pueblos.* These dwellings contained between 75 and 400 rooms clustered around open courtyards. One of the most famous of these villages is Pueblo Bonito in what is now Chaco Culture National Historical Park in New Mexico. Here the Anasazi built a 650-room complex, five stories high. An active trade network flourished among the many pueblos. About 400 miles of roads were laid to connect the villages.

As the population grew and food sources were depleted, widespread hunger resulted. Villagers began raiding one another for food. To protect themselves from attack, some moved into more remote areas of the canyons and began building their pueblos on the mesas. When tribes of warlike nomads came into the region, the Anasazi began building their multistoried dwellings inside the caves or under cliff overhangs on the steep sides of the mesas. These cliff dwellings were almost impossible to attack successfully.

Perched high on a cliff in central Arizona is Montezuma Castle. It was named by settlers who believed that the castle was built by Aztecs fleeing from Mexico. The castle has no connection with the Aztec emperor Montezuma.

The Cliff Dwellers

The Anasazi built hundreds of cliff dwellings throughout the canyons of the Four Corners region. Many of the sheer sandstone cliffs are thousands of feet high. The cliff pueblos were built from about 40 feet to several hundred feet from the cliff base, wherever there was a natural cave or shelter from the elements. These cliff dwellings ranged in size from a few rooms with only one *kiva* (ceremonial room) to large terraced structures with over 100 rooms and several kivas. The cliff "apartment buildings" varied in height from two to four stories. They were constructed with stones held together by adobe—a mixture of mud and thatch dried in the sun. Rooms, which were joined, had flat roofs and were circular or rectangular in shape. Builders constructed one room upon another, with the upper story a short distance back from the one below. The walls were smoothly plastered and decorated with red, yellow, black, and white designs.

To reach these cliff dwellings, the Anasazi often made a "hand-and-toe trail" by chipping foot-sized steps

The Cliff Palace at Mesa Verde, Colorado, is the largest and most famous of the cliff dwellings. Archaeologists found many artifacts at this site that provided clues about the lives of these prehistoric people.

into the steep canyon walls. Some dwellings could be reached only by using ladders, which were withdrawn once everyone was inside the pueblo or in the event of an attack.

Canyon de Chelly One of the best-known cliff dwellings is the White House in Canyon de Chelly National Monument, Arizona. Built around 1066, the White House's name comes from the upper part of the ruin, which is a long wall covered with white plaster. About 100 people occupied the White House.

Mesa Verde One of the largest cliff pueblos is Cliff Palace located in Mesa Verde National Park in Colorado. It was built into a tremendous cave in Cliff Canyon during the 12th century. There are 220 rooms, some of which are four stories high. The Mesa Verde complex contains 23 kivas and several pit houses for storage. Historians believe that as many as 400 people may have lived there.

Monuments to the Anasazi

In 1276, after years of below-normal rainfall, a serious drought struck the Four Corners region. The resulting disease and starvation, attacks from nomadic people, and internal quarreling forced the Anasazi to move east and south.

By the 1700s, members of the Hopi and Navajo tribes were living in some of the abandoned cliff dwellings. In 1864, frontiersman and scout Kit Carson and his troops forced the Navajo to leave the cliff dwellings. In 1868, some of the Navajo returned to the canyons but not to the cliff dwellings.

The first scientific exploration of the cliff sites began at Canyon de Chelly in 1873. Unfortunately, looters also arrived, disturbing many of the sites. By 1975, some 4,000 Anasazi sites had been found in the canyons of Mesa Verde alone. Archaeologists found undamaged clay pots and stone tools at the Cliff Palace site.

Today, the National Park Service preserves and protects many of these ancient Anasazi sites. Archaeological digs still are occurring at many canyon sites. Each year, thousands of tourists visit the Anasazi cliff dwellings in the Southwestern United States to marvel at the skill of these Native Americans.

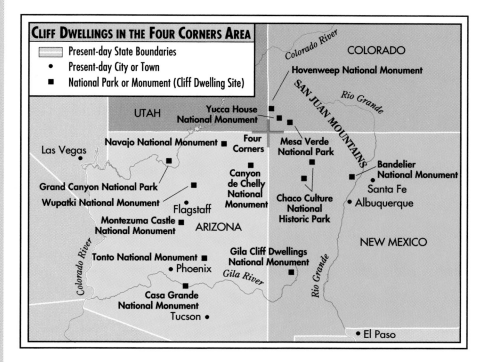

In the Four Corners region of the United States—where Arizona, New Mexico, Colorado, and Utah meet—there are hundreds of adobe dwellings and villages. Some are easy to reach. But others are in remote areas, reachable only on horseback or by hiking.

Chartres Cathedral

Famous for its
stained glass windows
and sculptures,
Chartres Cathedral
is considered
a masterpiece
of Gothic architecture.

This magnificent cathedral, towering above the city of Chartres, set the standard for later cathedrals.

The City of Chartres

The ancient city of Chartres is in north-central France, about 50 miles from Paris. For centuries, the life of the townspeople centered around the local church. In the late 9th century, the church received the gift of a holy relic—the veil of the Virgin Mary. As word of this gift spread throughout the Catholic world, hundreds of religious pilgrims came to Chartres to see the veil. The city prospered and became a famous religious center. By the 12th century, its religious school had gained world renown.

One of its teachers—Thierry of Chartres—proposed new ideas about the connection between the physical structure of a church or cathedral and its spiritual role. Thierry used geometry to support his theory. He theorized that the cross-shaped form of the building should represent the crucifixion of Christ. He saw the church as a "picture book" of the Bible. Through form and decoration, the church could teach religion. Since few people could read or write at that time, the church would be their teacher. Thierry's ideas became central to the development of a new style of architecture, which came to be called Gothic.

A New Style Emerges The Gothic style emerged during the late 1100s. It was a break with the Romanesque architecture, which had dominated church design. Romanesque buildings were solid, heavy-looking structures with thick walls, rounded arches, and sparse decoration. In contrast, the Gothic style emphasized:

- lightness and immense size;
- pointed arches and arcades;
- high vaulted (arched) ceilings with visible structural beams (ribs);
- high pointed spires;

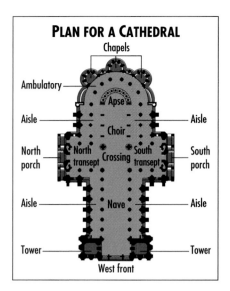

No matter where cathedrals were built or who built them, many have the same basic floor plan—the shape of a cross.

- flying buttresses—half-arch stone supports on the outer walls to bear the weight of the ceilings; and
- an abundance of decoration, including sculptures and stained glass windows.

Stained glass, held in place by decorative stonework, substituted for large sections of wall. Tall spires reached high into the air, suggesting closeness to God. The abundance of statues of saints was believed to protect the buildings they inhabited from harm.

The Great Cathedral Age The great Gothic cathedrals of France were built between 1150 and 1300, a period of peace and prosperity. Chartres Cathedral replaced several earlier churches that were built on the same site and destroyed by fire. Construction on the present cathedral began in 1194. Nobles, peasants, shopkeepers, and laborers came together to build the cathedral. It was as much a matter of civic pride as a religious tribute.

Form and Detail

The architect of Chartres Cathedral, whose name is unknown, designed a new structure adjoining the portion of the Romanesque cathedral that had survived the fire. Although the completed structure is actually a blend of two styles—Romanesque and Gothic—the cathedral has a feeling of unity. This unity is partly due to the fact that the structure was completed in a remarkably short time—31 years. Most cathedrals this size took much longer to construct, and many had more than one architect.

Towering high above the town, the cathedral has an interior height of more than 120 feet. Historians believe that construction proceeded from west to east, beginning with the Romanesque elements of the previous structure and giving way to Gothic elements of the new. The main *facade,* or face, of the cathedral consists of a triple doorway and two tall spires.

The long main section of the church, called the *nave,* is 52 feet wide—wider than that of any other French cathedral. On the floor is a mazelike design with 320 feet of winding passages, which the faithful followed on their knees.

Famous Windows The stained glass windows are the cathedral's sole source of natural light. The sun passing through the colored glass has been described as magical. It creates jewellike patterns on the stone interior. Because of the windows, the building has been called the "Cathedral of Light."

The oldest windows in the west front were in place before the Gothic cathedral was built. They are famous for their rich blues and wide floral borders. During the main construction, 176 stained glass windows covering

about 26,000 square feet of surface were added. Each of the rose windows, named for their shape and petallike forms that radiate from the center, measures about 40 feet in diameter. The west rose window details the life of Christ. The nave windows contain other religious scenes, decorative borders, and the coats of arms of noble families.

The beauty of the windows is even more remarkable because the artisans who made the glass worked in studios away from the cathedral. They did not see the finished windows until all the pieces were in place.

The stained glass windows of Chartres Cathedral are its only source of natural light.

Setting the Standard

Chartres Cathedral was dedicated in 1264, and many who entered truly felt that they were in a holy place. Chartres Cathedral set the standards for Gothic architecture throughout Europe. The great French cathedrals of Amiens and Reims were built during the period known as High Gothic which followed the completion of Chartres.

In the 14th century, a Chapter House, where church council meetings were held, was added. In 1836, fire destroyed the roof. It was replaced with a metal framework covered with copper, which is there today.

Chartres Cathedral is still a place of worship, as it has been for centuries. It also welcomes tourists from around the world who come to see and admire its Gothic majesty.

This list includes some of the largest and most beautiful cathedrals in the world.

MAJOR CATHEDRALS		
Cathedral	**Location**	**Date of Completion**
Hagia Sophia	Istanbul, Turkey	A.D. 537
Santiago de Compostela	Compostela, Spain	1128
Notre Dame de Paris	Paris, France	1250
Salisbury Cathedral	Wiltshire, England	1258
Chartres Cathedral	Chartres, France	1264
Seville Cathedral	Seville, Spain	1520
St. Basil's Cathedral	Moscow, Russia	1560
St. Paul's Cathedral	London, England	1710
Milan Cathedral	Milan, Italy	1813
Church of Notre Dame de Montreal	Montreal, Canada	1829
St. Patrick's Cathedral	New York, United States	1879
Cologne Cathedral	Cologne, Germany	1880

The Dikes of the Netherlands

Through a system of flood barriers, the Dutch have reclaimed land from the sea.

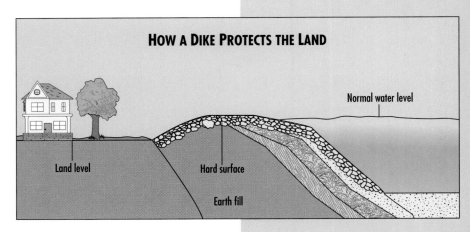

HOW A DIKE PROTECTS THE LAND

Normal water level

Land level

Hard surface

Earth fill

The top of a sea dike is usually 10 to 16 feet above storm flood level. The outer, or ocean-facing, wall of a dike is reinforced with stone or concrete blocks. Still, the sea sometimes breaks through.

The Lowlands

When the first permanent settlements were established in the Netherlands 6,000 years ago, the land was mostly marshes and shallow lakes. About one-half of the country was below sea level, which accounts for its name— Netherlands means "lowlands."

About 2,500 years ago, the Frisians built great mounds of earth and clay in the northwestern region. These early people came from islands along the coast of the Netherlands, Germany, and Denmark. Descendants of the Frisians still live in the Netherlands. On these mounds, which were called *terpen,* the people built their homes and other buildings. Some terpen were so large that entire villages were constructed on them. The Frisians also developed a system of walls to keep the sea out. Made of stone and dirt, these seawalls were the country's first dikes.

In 58 B.C., the Romans conquered the region and controlled it for the next 400 years. They built dikes along the seacoast and dams along the region's rivers. Many cities—such as Amsterdam, Rotterdam, Zaandam, and Edam—grew up around these water barriers.

Taming the Sea

Throughout the centuries, the Dutch have struggled to secure themselves against floods caused by North Sea storms. Over the years, they developed a special way of classifying the dikes, based on age and location. A "watcher" dike is the newest dike and serves as the first line of defense from the sea. A "dreamer" dike is farther inland and older than a watcher. A "sleeper" dike is still farther inland. The oldest dike in an area, and the one farthest inland, is a "dead" dike. As more land is reclaimed from the sea, a new watcher is built. This new dike, in turn, makes the old watcher a dreamer, the old dreamer a sleeper, and so on.

In the past, whenever floods threatened, the town declared a "dike peace." All arguments between neighbors were put aside, and the townspeople worked together to reinforce the dikes.

Building a Dike To construct a dike, workers first made huge "mattresses" of brushwood, sand, and gravel. Several acres in size, these mats were the foundations for the earthen dikes. Workers floated the mattresses to where the dike was needed and sank them with stones. Then sand and clay were loaded onto these sunken mats until a new dike

In the early 1950s, the sea broke through the dike near Terneuzen, flooding the land on the other side.

To create habitable land, water had to be removed or brought under control. Enough water was left in this polder to ensure its availability for irrigation.

formed. Although machinery and materials have changed over the centuries, the process for building dikes remains the same.

Reclaiming the Land By the 17th century, the people had secured their country from the worst North Sea storms. They then turned their attention to expanding their territory by converting sea area to land area. These reclaimed land areas are called *polders*. To create a polder, an area is encircled by earthen dikes. Then the water is removed from that area. Power generated by windmills was used to pump water from the polder. Between 1200 and 1400, hundreds of windmills were built for this purpose. The wind turned large sails on the windmill, which turned a scooper. The scooper lifted water from the polder and hurled it across the dike. Today, electrically powered pumps remove water from the polders by raising it to a ring canal, which leads the excess water to the sea by way of a trough.

Through the construction of dikes and the creation of polders, the country has almost doubled its land area over the centuries. The people who live there say that "God created the world, but the Dutch created [the Netherlands]."

Despite the efforts of the Dutch to maintain and repair existing dikes, storms from the North Sea have broken through from time to time. In the 13th century, terrible floods created a large inland sea, which residents named the Zuider Zee. Many attempts were made to reclaim the land. But none succeeded until 1932. That year, the Dutch built a huge dike—25 feet high and more than 20 miles long—and closed off the Zuider Zee. Since then, more than 700 square miles of the surrounding land have been drained to create several large polders.

World War II Destruction The Germans occupied the Netherlands during much of World War II. To hinder the advance of Allied troops from the United States, France, and Great Britain, the Germans flooded some of the polders. Their occupation of the Dutch city of Walcheren closed the nearby port of Antwerp, Belgium. To open the port, the Allies bombed the dikes around Walcheren and flushed the Germans from the city. After the war, the Allied countries helped to rebuild the dikes and drain the polders.

Recent Developments

The fortification of existing dikes and the building of new ones continues throughout the Netherlands. In 1953, a terrible storm smashed through the dikes in the southern part of Holland, drowning over 1,800 people. To protect the southwestern part of the country from future storm disasters, the Dutch government established the Delta Project. About 20 miles of new dikes have been built to date. Modern highways, linked by a series of bridges, were constructed on top of the dikes. One part of the project, the Oosterschelde Barrier, was completed in 1986. It is the world's largest sea barrier. It is designed to close when severe storms threaten the southern region. Because of the tremendous size of the barrier and the dangerous tidal currents of the river it crosses, it took nine years to build. But the effort paid off. When seven terrible storms threatened to flood the area in 1990, the barrier protected the region from flood damage.

The Netherlands is famous for its dikes. They have been the subject of many stories. But only the Dutch truly understand how important they are as protective barriers and as a means for creating habitable land.

During severe weather or very high tides, the Oosterschelde Barrier is closed to protect the nearby land.

The Alhambra

The last stronghold of the Moors in Spain, this palace-fortress is the finest example of Islamic art in Europe.

The Fortress at Granada

The ancient city of Granada in southern Spain is nestled among the Sierra Nevada mountains. It is surrounded by rich valleys and the fertile slopes of the Sierra foothills. A rocky plateau high above the city forms a natural fortress. Throughout history, this plateau has been fortified by various conquerors to protect Granada.

Muslims from North Africa, called Moors, invaded Spain in the early 8th century. During the 9th century, they built a small fortress, called the Alcazaba, on the plateau above Granada. Because this fort had pink-tinged walls, they called it the *Al-Qal'a al-Hamra,* which means "the Red House," and which the Spanish called Alhambra.

The Nasrid Dynasty By 1238, the Moors had been driven from all of Spain, with the exception of Andalusia, a region in southern Spain. In that year, the Nasrid Dynasty rose to power in Andalusia and ruled until 1492. The royal court was located at Granada. The court of the Kingdom of Granada was famous for its scholars and artists. The artistry of the Moors reached its peak with the building of the Alhambra.

The first Nasrid rulers made improvements to the Alhambra. They constructed aqueducts to bring water to the fortress, and they built strong walls encircling the top of the plateau. They strategically placed 24 towers around the walls.

Moorish Splendor

The palace of the Alhambra is one of the world's architectural and artistic masterpieces. It is a complex of magnificent halls, rooms, courtyards, orchards, and gardens tucked behind the plain walls of the 35-acre fortress. Sultans Yusuf I and Mohammed V built the palace during the 13th and 14th centuries.

Although the Alhambra does not have a formal plan, the overall feeling is one of harmony. Everything is linked by the grouping of rooms around the two principal courtyards—the Court of the Lions and the Court of the Myrtles. The Alhambra is structured in such a way that one spectacular view unfolds onto another, as archways open into courtyards, corridors, and windowed halls. A building device characteristic of the Alhambra is the *mirador,* a small enclosed space that provides a different perspective from each of its arched openings.

Because the Moors were descended from desert peoples, they considered water a luxury. Therefore, they included water and luscious vegetation in their construction. The palace is filled with fountains, ornamental pools, and baths. The baths are decorated with blue, green, yellow, and white mosaic tiles. Beautiful plants and flowers adorn the courtyards. Moorish architecture is light and open, with delicate details and interwoven shapes and patterns.

Artistic Originality The artists used elaborate geometric and floral designs in stone, plaster, and ceramic tiles to decorate the palace. Archways are framed by delicate, lacelike plasterwork designs. Ornamental inscriptions from the Koran, the sacred book of Islam, also are used as decoration.

Like many other structures that began as fortresses, the Alhambra was built on a hill. From here, the inhabitants could spot invaders early.

The Alhambra is known for its unusual ceiling ornamentations, called stalactites. These are lacy, icicle-shaped forms carved in plaster or stone, which are clustered to create intricate, honeycomb patterns. The domed ceiling of the Hall of the Two Sisters has stalactites arranged in beautiful, multicolored patterns.

Court of the Lions The famous Court of the Lions was reserved for use by the royal family. It provided a quiet, beautiful place in which to stroll and think. The courtyard is circled by an arcade of horseshoe arches of richly decorated plasterwork. Colorful mosaic tiles cover the lower half of the gallery (passageway) walls. In the center is an alabaster fountain supported by 12 marble lions. This courtyard is a perfect blend of sunlight, water, foliage, and handcrafted decoration.

Court of the Myrtles This courtyard is named for the hedges of myrtle that line the sides of a rectangular pool—150 feet in length—in the center of the yard. The entrances to the court are framed by arcades. These arcades are composed of a series of arches upheld by columns that look like palm trees. Lacy plasterwork adorns the arches and the galleries. The still water in the pool reflects the magnificence of the artwork.

Hall of the Ambassadors The largest room in the palace—the Hall of the Ambassadors—served as the throne room and the place where the sultan received visitors. It has a domed ceiling and a tower rising over it. The hall was designed to show the power and majesty of the Moorish court. Ornamental quotations from the Koran frame the arched entrances.

In the peaceful atmosphere of the Court of the Lions, the royal family could sit or stroll and escape the heavy burdens of government.

The Fall of the Moors

Spanish Christians fought for almost 800 years to reclaim their land from the Islamic Moors. Finally, in 1492, the last of the Moorish rulers in Spain surrendered at Granada to the Catholic monarchs Ferdinand and Isabella. The Spanish did not destroy the fortress-palace of the Alhambra, in part because of their admiration for it as a work of art.

In the 16th century, a section of the Alhambra was demolished to make room for a palace for Charles, king of Spain and Holy Roman Emperor. Built between the Lion and Myrtle courts, Charles's palace was never completed. However, the finished portion shows a sharp contrast in style to the Moorish design. Charles's palace is symmetrical in design. Its massive columns give a feeling of heaviness and permanence.

During the 18th and early 19th centuries, the Alhambra suffered the effects of neglect, war, and earthquake damage. At times, it was inhabited only by gypsies. In the late 1800s, the palace was "discovered" by tourists. One visitor, American writer Washington Irving, wrote a book about the Alhambra. It became a popular subject for artists and writers. The palace has been partially restored. Today, thousands of tourists come to Granada for the sole purpose of savoring the splendor of this Islamic masterpiece.

Some of the finest examples of Islamic art, such as the carving shown here, are in the Alhambra.

The Taj Mahal

Known as
the White Jewel,
this famous tomb is a
timeless memorial to
a great love story.

The Mogul Empire

In the 16th century, the Moguls from Mongolia invaded northern India. By the 17th century, they had built an empire of fabulous wealth and power in India. The Mogul emperor had absolute power and was considered the link between God and humankind. A "throne or coffin" law (a fight to the death between brothers) determined succession. Emperors engaged in frequent military campaigns to gain territory, and they were very cruel to their enemies. The Moguls, who were Muslims, enjoyed savage sports and indulged in very extravagant pleasures. Many artists and craftspeople thrived, as beautiful objects were much in demand.

Love Story In 1607, according to legend, the 16-year-old son of Emperor Jahangir was strolling through a bazaar, where he saw the 15-year-old daughter of a high government official. They instantly fell in love. The prince asked his father for permission to marry her. Although marriages at that time usually were arranged for political or economic reasons, the emperor gave permission. However, the young lovers had to wait five years before their marriage took place. During that time, they never met or spoke to each other, and the prince married a Persian princess for political reasons. But Muslim law allowed a man to have four wives, so the prince could still marry his love. The couple married in 1612. The emperor was so enchanted by his son's new wife that he gave her the highest of honors—a new name. She became known as Mumtaz Mahal, which means the "Chosen One of the Palace."

The Rule of Shah Jahan In 1628, the prince became emperor and was henceforth called Shah Jahan, which means "King of the World." He reigned for 30 peaceful and prosperous years. The arts flourished during this time, and Shah Jahan built many elaborate monuments.

Mumtaz became a wise political adviser to her husband, ruling almost as his equal. She was admired for her compassion toward the poor, and poets wrote of her great beauty. She gave birth to 14 children, but only 7 survived. Mumtaz died in childbirth in 1631. Shah Jahan was overcome with grief and locked himself away for eight days with nothing to eat or drink. When he came out, he had been physically changed. According to legend, his hair was snow-white, and his back was permanently bent. He then ordered the entire empire into mourning for two years. He also decided to build a great monument to symbolize his love for Mumtaz.

Probably one of the most famous buildings in the world, the Taj Mahal is a monument to a great love story.

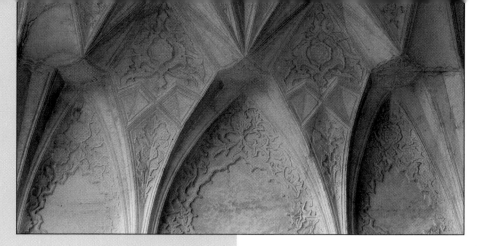

The White Jewel

Shah Jahan chose a site along the banks of the sacred Jumna River near the royal city of Agra to build his monument. He assembled a team of 37 of the finest artists, architects, engineers, and craftspeople from all over East Asia to design and build the Taj Mahal, which means "Crown of the Queen." It took 20,000 men and women 22 years to build this impressive work of art. During this time, a small city grew up near the tomb site to house the workers. Agra became one of the great creative centers of the world.

Building the Taj For the construction itself, precious materials—such as jade and crystal—were gathered from all over the world. To transport marble blocks from the quarries to the site, the workers built an earthen ramp that ran ten miles—right through the city. Elephants and oxen dragged the marble along this ramp.

The tomb itself is made of gleaming white marble that seems to change color during the course of the day. Its exterior and interior surfaces are *mosaics,* designs inlaid with 43 varieties of gemstones in mortar. Intricate handwritten inscriptions frame the entrances.

Special Features The main feature is an enormous dome, which the Moslems consider to be the most perfect earthly form. A solid silver gate marks the entrance to the burial chamber. Fine mosaics—considered by some to be the best in the world—cover the casket. A delicately carved marble screen surrounds the casket.

In addition to the tomb itself, the monument contains a mosque on either side of the tomb and four slender towers—called minarets—attached to the mosques. The mosques are made of red sandstone and have three small domes apiece. The marble minarets are set on octagonal bases and taper to a height of 138 feet. They are crowned by a small domelike structure, called a cupola. From balconies on the minarets, criers call the people to prayer.

The complex also includes a huge gateway, walled gardens, and several smaller structures. Visitors enter the gardens through a large outer gate. Like other elements of the Taj Mahal, the gardens are divided into four square sections. (Four is the holiest number in the Islamic religion.) For Muslims, the entrance through the gardens to the Taj symbolizes the entrance into paradise.

Among the special features of the Taj Mahal is the delicately carved marble, such as this vaulted ceiling.

Monument to Love and Art

Shah Jahan assigned 2,000 soldiers to guard the grounds, and he held memorial services here every year. He intended to build his own tomb of black marble on the other side of the river with a silver bridge connecting it to the Taj. However, his son Alamgir seized power in 1658, before the tomb could be built. Shah Jahan was imprisoned at Agra until he died eight years later. His son buried him next to Mumtaz in the Taj Mahal.

The Mogul Empire fell to invaders in the mid-1700s. The tomb was plundered, and its decorations—gold lamps, silver candlesticks, gold handrails, and valuable Persian carpets—were carried away. The Taj Mahal lay neglected for 200 years, and the gardens became overgrown.

In 1858, Great Britain became the governing power in India. A plan to dismantle the tomb and ship the marble to England failed. However, the fabulous monument was used by the British for dances and picnics. In 1899, Lord Curzon, the British viceroy in India, ordered its restoration. It became the romantic subject of poems, tales, and paintings. Since India's independence in 1947, the Taj Mahal has been a major tourist attraction.

The mosaics that cover the interior and exterior surfaces of the tombs were made of gemstones set in mortar.

The Suez Canal

Since its construction, this artificial waterway has been of economic, political, and strategic importance.

With determination, Ferdinand de Lesseps overcame objections and obstacles and completed the Suez Canal in ten years.

Egypt and the Canal

The idea of canals to link the seas bordering Egypt dates back to ancient times. Early Egyptians built canals from the Nile River to the Red Sea. During the 7th century A.D., there was even a canal that connected the Mediterranean and Red seas. When Napoleon I invaded Egypt in 1798, he surveyed the Isthmus of Suez for a possible canal route.

In 1833, French diplomat and canal builder Ferdinand de Lesseps revived Napoleon's plan. De Lesseps saw the canal project as a way to break down barriers that "divide men, races, and nations." Permission for the project came from the ruler of Egypt, Said Pasha, in 1854. The following year, the International Technical Commission met to plan the canal route. In 1858, the Suez Canal Company was established to finance the project through the sale of stock, most of which was bought by the French and the Ottoman Turks. Said Pasha agreed to supply the workers.

Political problems arose when Great Britain opposed the project. By creating a shortcut to the East, the proposed canal would affect the profitable trade route around Africa's Cape of Good Hope, which Britain controlled. De Lesseps managed to overcome all objections, and the project moved ahead.

Joining the Seas

Canal construction began in 1859 and was completed in 1869. The narrow waterway extends about 118 miles north and south across the Isthmus of Suez. The canal is wide at the surface, then slopes downward to a narrow channel. It is a sea level canal with no locks, since the difference in the levels of the Mediterranean and Red seas is minimal.

A Great Engineering Achievement

Work began at Port Said on the Mediterranean with the construction of an artificial harbor and a freshwater reservoir to supply drinking water for the workers. Next, a preliminary ditch, or service canal, was dug to lay out the route of the proposed canal and provide a way to float supplies and machinery to the work areas. The first 30 miles of the canal from Port Said were dug through a marshy lagoon called Lake Manzala. To shore up the walls of the canal, workers laid chunks of mud on the ground to harden in the sun.

Natural obstacles along the route—such as the Sinai desert, rocky ridges, and five dry, salt-encrusted desert lakes—made the work more difficult. Careful planning and hard work overcame these obstacles.

The desert presented special problems. For example, winds deposited sand into the canal, which had to be dredged continually.

Money and Labor Problems At about the midpoint in the construction, the project faced bankruptcy. De Lesseps pressured Egypt into providing the necessary funds. At about the same time, international objections were raised regarding the use of forced labor. In 1865, the Egyptian government stopped this practice and hired workers from outside Egypt. These workers were paid in accordance with the amount they dug each day. Between 25,000 and 50,000 workers were employed on the project. They dug out a total of 97 million cubic yards of earth. Many died from the intense heat, overwork, and disease.

At first, workers were equipped with only shovels and baskets to fill with sand. When more money became available, machines were brought in to speed up the digging. Most of these machines, such as a mechanical dredger, were invented specifically for the Suez project. The dredger, placed on a barge in the canal, was operated by steam engines. An endless chain of buckets scooped up mud from the canal bottom and deposited it on the banks through long chutes.

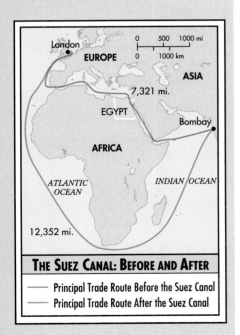

THE SUEZ CANAL: BEFORE AND AFTER

— Principal Trade Route Before the Suez Canal
— Principal Trade Route After the Suez Canal

The Canal's Importance

In 1869, the canal opened with a great celebration. A boat carrying de Lesseps and French empress Eugénie led a convoy of 50 ships through the canal. The canal had a major effect on commerce for the next century. It reduced the distance between England and India by about 5,000 miles. As a result, it became the busiest interocean waterway in the world. Egypt benefited in many ways from the Suez Canal. The freshwater reservoirs that had been built for the workers could now be used for irrigation, reclaiming much desert land for farming. Prosperous new towns grew up along the canal.

Almost immediately, the canal was found to be too narrow. It has been deepened and enlarged many times, beginning with the first expansion in 1875. Today, the canal's depth is 64 feet. Its width is 302 feet at the bottom and 741 feet at the surface. The canal also needs frequent dredging since desert winds fill it with sand. The passage through the canal is time-consuming, with single-lane traffic over much of its length. Experienced pilots guide the convoys of ships.

The canal had special importance for Great Britain, helping that nation to maintain its empire. In 1875, Britain purchased the Egyptian ruler's shares in the canal. After that, a commission consisting of French and British investors took over the management of the canal.

By an international agreement signed in 1888, the canal was opened

Before the building of the Suez Canal, British trading ships had to sail around the African continent to reach India. The canal shortened that distance by about 5,000 miles.

The canal has been widened several times. Today, it can accommodate large cargo ships, such as this one.

to all nations. Although the Suez Canal remained open during both world wars, only Britain's allies could use it.

Suez Crisis In 1956, the Egyptian government headed by Gamal Abdel Nasser seized and nationalized the canal. France, Britain, and Israel attacked Egypt to try to restore international control of the canal. The United Nations intervened, and the canal was reopened under Egyptian control in 1957.

Arab-Israeli Conflict Between 1967 and 1975, the Suez Canal again was closed—this time due to two wars between Egypt and Israel. Israeli ships were barred from using the canal until 1978. In that year, Egyptian president Anwar Sadat and Israeli prime minister Menachem Begin signed an historic peace treaty ending a 30-year-old conflict between their two nations.

In 1980, a tunnel was completed under the canal. The tunnel, which is ten miles north of the city of Suez, is for cars and trucks. Today, the canal is still a shipping route of major international importance.

The Statue of Liberty

Once the tallest monument in the world, this gift from France has become an international symbol of freedom.

France and the United States

In 1776, the French government supported the American colonists in their fight for independence from Great Britain. Then in 1789, the French fought their own revolution for freedom and equality. Although the dictatorship of Napoleon I interrupted the revolution, many French people continued to dream of liberty. They carefully monitored the democratic experiment in the United States.

By 1865, France was under the repressive rule of Napoleon III, and the United States had reaffirmed its democracy by defeating the Confederacy and freeing the slaves. At about that time, French political scholar and historian Édouard Laboulaye proposed an idea to friends at a dinner party. He suggested building a monument to liberty for the United States. He saw this idea as a way to celebrate the friendship between the two countries. It also would be a way for the French people to show their support for freedom of thought and religious tolerance, which were restricted in their own country.

Sculptor Frédéric Auguste Bartholdi was another guest at the party. He liked Laboulaye's idea and suggested that the monument be a colossal statue.

Liberty in History The ancient Romans had built a temple to the Goddess of Liberty, which began the tradition of depicting Liberty as a robed woman wearing a cap. Bartholdi modified this representation when he designed his statue. In place of the cap, he designed a crown with seven points to symbolize the seven continents and seven seas. In one hand of the statue, he placed a torch, or, as he called it, a "beacon of enlightenment" to represent knowledge and truth. In Liberty's other hand, he placed a tablet inscribed with the date of U.S. independence from England. He made several models of the statue, completing the first model in 1870 and the final model in 1876.

Frédéric Auguste Bartholdi envisioned a statue that would be "Grand as the idea which it embodies [liberty], radiant upon the two worlds [France and the United States]."

Before the statue was assembled in New York, the arm and torch were displayed in Philadelphia.

Lady Liberty

At first, neither the American public nor the government was enthusiastic about the proposed statue. Nevertheless, Bartholdi came to the United States to select a site for the statue. He picked the 12-acre Bedloe's Island in New York City's harbor. By 1877, Congress had agreed to accept the gift of the Statue of Liberty. A committee was formed in the United States to raise funds for the statue's base and pedestal, which the U.S. government had agreed to provide.

The French quickly raised the money for the statue's construction. However, contributions in the United States lagged until 1885, when publishing giant Joseph Pulitzer raised much of the money through a campaign in his New York newspaper, *The World*.

Building the Statue Construction of the statue itself occurred in France; the base and pedestal were built in America. In addition to the

Full-sized plaster models of parts of the statue were made. Negative wooden forms were built around the plaster, reversing the statue's contours.

Symbol of Freedom

This colossal monument was unveiled in 1886. Although the statue was originally called "Liberty Enlightening the World," it became known as the Statue of Liberty almost immediately. The statue was the first sight for millions of immigrants who sailed into New York harbor in the late 1800s.

Each year, about two million people take the boat ride from lower Manhattan or New Jersey to Bedloe's Island (renamed Liberty Island by Congress in 1956) to visit the Statue of Liberty. Many visitors climb the 142 steps up a double spiral staircase to Liberty's head and crown. The view of New York and the Hudson River is spectacular from the crown.

By 1980, the skeletal iron rods had reacted with the copper skin, causing serious erosion. During the major restoration project in the mid-1980s, the iron rods were replaced with stainless steel. The pedestal, the base, and the torch flame were repaired. In 1986, the Statue of Liberty celebrated its centennial. Today, it remains a powerful symbol of freedom and hope in the world.

project's originator and the statue's sculptor, many others were involved in the project. They included:

- Gustave Eiffel, the French engineer who designed the supporting iron framework;
- Civil War veteran General Charles P. Stone, who supervised construction of the base; and
- Richard Morris Hunt, the American architect who designed the pedestal.

In 1876, the statue's right hand—holding the torch of liberty—was finished and displayed at the Philadelphia Centennial Exhibition. It was then displayed in Madison Square Park in New York City as a publicity stunt to raise money. In 1878, Liberty's head was completed and exhibited at the Paris International Fair.

Iron Frame and Copper Skin

Gustave Eiffel's framework for the statue was a central iron tower to be anchored in the pedestal. He then constructed a secondary structure in the general shape of the statue. Next he hung a series of flat, springy iron bars from it. These would eventually connect to the statue's outer "skin."

In sculpting the statue, Bartholdi first made a series of clay models of increasing size. Then craftsmen made full-scale plaster copies and surrounded them with wooden frames. The thin copper sheets that make up the outer skin of the statue were formed by beating them into shape inside the wooden frames. Workers then joined the 300 overlapping sections of hammered copper frame using 300,000 rivets.

Following the presentation of the statue to the United States in Paris in 1884, it was dismantled, crated, and shipped to America. In the United States, the reconstruction of the statue on its pedestal began. Laborers worked from the bottom up, without using any exterior scaffolding.

The statue itself is 152 feet high; the pedestal is 89 feet high on a 65-foot-high base. Although the statue weighs 225 tons, its construction allows for a sway of as much as three inches in the winds that whip around New York City's harbor. Liberty's mouth (three feet wide) and her index finger (eight feet long) underscore her enormous size.

A major restoration of the Statue of Liberty occurred in the mid-1980s.

The Eiffel Tower

Designed by Gustave Eiffel, France's best-known landmark was once described as a "stairway to the sky."

Many people doubted that Eiffel's design could be implemented. The first platform and rigid base assured the doubters that there was enough support for the final structure.

Iron Master

Alexandre Gustave Eiffel was born in Dijon, France, in 1832. He studied metal construction as a youth and opened his own metalworks in a Paris suburb in 1876. He became famous for his wrought iron structures. This type of iron is tough and rust-resistant. It also can be hammered into various shapes without breaking.

Gustave Eiffel had a degree in chemistry. But a job offer from a company that manufactured railway equipment convinced him to give up chemistry for civil engineering.

Eiffel built domes, roofs, and bridges. When his Garabit railroad bridge over the Truyère River in southern France was completed in 1882, it was the highest arched bridge in the world. He even created the metal framework for the Statue of Liberty in New York's harbor.

Paris Exposition In the late 1880s, France began planning for the 1889 Exposition to be held in Paris. The Exposition coincided with the 100th anniversary of the French Revolution. The planners wanted a special monument to celebrate the revolution and to be the central attraction of the Exposition. Many designs were submitted; Gustave Eiffel's design was chosen. He proposed to build the world's tallest structure. At that time, the Washington Monument in Washington, D.C., was the tallest at 554 feet.

Eiffel's design for an iron tower provoked much controversy. Some critics tried to stop its construction, saying that it would be an eyesore and a dishonor to Paris. Others called the tower a "tragic lamppost" and an "inverted torch-holder."

Creation of a Landmark

Eiffel disregarded the negative opinions and proceeded with his plan—to build a 984-foot wrought iron tower. (In hot weather, the tower actually is seven inches higher because of the expansion of the metal.)

Eiffel was under much pressure to finish the tower in time for the Exposition. He decided to build a lightweight tower of wrought iron ribs held together by rivets. The structure would rest on a masonry foundation.

The tower was built between 1887 and 1889 by a workforce of 230 men. About 100 laborers worked in the factory to make the parts. The remaining workers assembled those parts at the construction site. The finished tower weighed 9,547 tons and consisted of 18,000 components held together by 2.5 million rivets.

Eiffel's Innovation One of Eiffel's most important accomplishments was his innovative construction technique. He used prefabricated components that were designed and made elsewhere. The many parts were brought to the site and put together, piece by piece, from the foundation up. This prefabrication technique enabled the crews to work faster and complete the tower in time for the Exposition.

The 50 engineers on the project had made 5,300 drawings showing the precise location of the holes in the component sections. Off-site, workers drilled seven million holes in the structure's sections. On-site, other workers riveted these sections together using portable forges. Under the leadership of Gustave Eiffel, the work was so accurate that, as the tower rose, the prefabricated parts fit together perfectly. Another remarkable accomplishment was that not one worker lost his life building the tower.

From the Foundation Up To create the solid masonry foundation for the tower, huge steel containers called caissons were sunk into the ground and filled with concrete. Each of these caissons was 50 feet long, 22 feet wide, and 7 feet deep. Four gigantic legs stood on these concrete and steel foundations, each composed of four columns. Hydraulic jacks at the base of these columns were used to raise or lower the legs. All four had to be exactly the same height to support the framework for the next stage of the tower. Atop these legs, Eiffel placed the tower's first platform. Once it was securely in place, cranes were lifted onto it, and parts were raised for the next stage. In this way, the tower kept growing.

Designed for Visitors The Eiffel Tower has always been operated as a commercial enterprise. Two double-deck elevators were installed to carry visitors to the various stages of the tower. One elevator took sightseers to the first platform. The other took people from ground level to the second platform. The elevators had enough seats in them to accommodate about 50 people per trip.

This "ridiculous dizzy tower," as some critics called it, became France's most famous landmark and one of the most distinctive towers in the world.

Stairway to the Sky

On March 31, 1889, a small group of dignitaries climbed the 1,792 steps to the top of the Eiffel Tower to hoist a huge French flag. Meanwhile, on the ground, tables were laid for a celebration. Among the celebrants were the engineers, the workers, the prime minister, and other invited guests.

Now that the tower was up, many critics found it much more stately than they had predicted. Despite its massive iron content, it had a remarkable lightness and gracefulness. The tower was an enormous hit at the Paris Exposition, attracting almost two million visitors during the last five months of 1889 alone. People paid two francs to ascend to the first platform, another franc to continue to the second level, and two more francs to go to the top. By the end of 1889, 75 percent of the total cost to build the tower had been recovered.

The Eiffel Tower was intended to last only 20 years. The fact that it has lasted for more than a century is a tribute to Gustave Eiffel and his ingenious design. The tower still attracts millions of visitors each year.

During the 1980s, the Eiffel Tower underwent a major face-lift that cost $28 million. Excess weight, such as a 590-foot circular staircase that was added after the tower's completion, was removed. The Eiffel Tower is painted every seven years—using 45 tons of paint each time.

From the top of the tower, visitors have a spectacular view of Paris. The Eiffel Tower has attracted many publicity seekers. In 1983, two cyclists rode trail bikes up the stairs to the second platform and safely down again. Despite increased security, a British couple slipped past security guards and parachuted from the top in 1984. French authorities were not amused.

Hoover Dam

The highest concrete arch dam in the United States, it has had an enormous effect on the growth of the Southwest.

River of Life

The Colorado River runs through or along the border of five Western states and Mexico. Early settlers of the land bordering the Colorado depended on the river for drinking water and irrigation. After heavy rains, the Colorado overflowed its banks, leaving behind rich topsoil that was ideal for farming. At other times, long periods of drought depleted the river.

Flood Damage For years, farmers looked for ways to control the flow of water. In 1902, the Imperial Canal was completed, bringing water from the Colorado to California's Imperial Valley. However, in 1905, the rampaging river broke through the canal's diversion controls and flooded the valley. Alternating periods of flood and drought followed this disaster, causing serious damage to this rich agricultural area. Farmers then tried a system of levees, embankments built to control the flooding. Some levees were earthen banks along the river to keep high water from flooding the neighboring land. Others were low ridges of earth around a farm field. The levee system was unsatisfactory because it did nothing to lessen the effects of drought.

By the early 1920s, people realized that a dam on the Colorado River was needed to control the flooding and drought cycle. But conflicts arose over the purpose of the dam—whether to provide water for drinking and irrigation or to provide hydroelectric power to the region. Hydroelectric power is electricity produced by converting the energy of running water.

Boulder Canyon Project The U.S. Congress authorized the Boulder Canyon Project in 1928. It was a mammoth project and had three main purposes: to control floods, to generate electricity, and to provide for the storage and delivery of water to the region. The plan called for a dam, a hydroelectric power plant, and a reservoir. Although the project was ambitious and expensive (costing about $385 million) members of Congress felt that the dam eventually would pay for itself through the fees collected for the use of the hydroelectric power.

The dam was designed by the Bureau of Reclamation, a government agency set up in 1902 to develop water and land resources in the West. Construction began in 1931 in the Black Canyon, about 25 miles southeast of Las Vegas. The project was called Boulder Dam by those who worked on it.

A Great Dam Rises

Engineers designed an arched dam, the type usually built in narrow canyons. This semicircular shape gives the dam extra strength because, as the water pushes against the dam, the arch shifts the force of the water outward toward the canyon walls. Hoover Dam is the highest concrete arched dam in the United States, and one of the highest concrete dams in the world.

- The dam is 725 feet high and 1,244 feet long.
- Its base is 660 feet thick.
- Over 4.4 million cubic yards of concrete were used in its construction. (That same amount of concrete could pave a two-lane highway from coast to coast.)
- Elevators descend to a depth of more than 44 stories before reaching the base.
- The dam has 17 huge water-driven turbines (engines) generating electric power.

The reservoir created by the dam, called Lake Mead, is approximately 115 miles long. One of the world's largest artificially created bodies of water, Lake Mead is 589 feet deep and has a storage capacity of billions of gallons of water.

Hoover Dam, the highest arched dam in the world, took five years to construct.

Tourists watch the awesome power of the Colorado River waters overflow the spillways at Hoover Dam.

The Effect of Hoover Dam

Hoover Dam—as it came to be called—with its reservoir and power plant, contributed much to the growth of the southwestern United States. It provided inexpensive electric power and a dependable supply of water to towns in southern California.

Water from Lake Mead is used to irrigate about one million acres of farmland in Nevada, Arizona, and California. The reservoir also supplies drinking water—transported along 240 miles of aqueduct—for cities in southern California.

The Hoover Dam power plant is one of the most important sources of hydroelectric power in the world. The electricity produced by the 17 generators in the power plant is sold to industries, towns, and cities throughout the Southwest.

In 1947, Congress officially renamed the dam Hoover Dam, in honor of Herbert Hoover, who was President when the project began. Because of its immense size and dramatic setting, Hoover Dam has become a major tourist attraction.

People can take a short car ride from Las Vegas, then walk along the dam's crest and descend into its cavern. There they can watch the water falling through the huge turbines. Lake Mead, declared a national recreational area by act of Congress, is a popular spot for tourists and sailing enthusiasts.

Era of Dam Building The 20th century was a period of major dam construction around the world. Many regions recognized the value of dams for generating relatively inexpensive hydroelectric power and for providing a dependable water supply.

The Grand Coulee Dam soon surpassed the Hoover Dam in terms of hydroelectric capacity. Located on the Columbia River in the state of Washington, it is 550 feet high and 4,173 feet long. Grand Coulee was built to generate electricity for the region and to irrigate over one million acres of desert land.

Another great dam is the Itaipu Dam, completed in 1984. Located on the Paraná River on the Paraguay-Brazil border, it is the world's most powerful dam, with 18 turbines generating electricity.

Although these dams have surpassed Hoover in size and power-generating capacity, Hoover Dam's importance continues as a model for arched dam design and for its effect on the development and prosperity of the region it serves.

Lake Mead, the reservoir for Hoover Dam, was the first national recreation area established by an act of Congress.

The Golden Gate Bridge

Once called "the bridge that could never be," this remarkable steel span has become a symbol for the city of San Francisco.

San Francisco

Located on a narrow peninsula between the Pacific Ocean and San Francisco Bay, the city of San Francisco was built on a series of hills near the foothills of the beautiful Sierra Nevada mountains. Some residents dreamed of a bridge across the bay linking the city to the California counties to the north. The devastating 1906 earthquake and the need to rebuild the city occupied San Franciscans for a time. But by 1918, the idea of the bridge had revived.

A resolution to build a bridge across the Golden Gate—the two-mile-wide channel at the entrance to San Francisco Bay—was put before city leaders. The city engineer objected because such a project would encounter tremendous problems—the extraordinary depth and width of the bay, the very strong currents, and the high winds. But Richard J. Welch, the project's most enthusiastic supporter, would not give up. He soon found an important ally in Joseph Strauss, an engineer.

Chief Engineer Joseph Strauss had already designed more than 500 bridges in the United States and overseas. The special problems posed by the Golden Gate intrigued him. He was sure that a bridge across the channel could be built, and he proceeded to design such a bridge. Following approval of Strauss's design by the California legislature in 1923, the Golden Gate Bridge and Highway District was created to manage the construction of the bridge. In 1929, Strauss was appointed chief engineer. Public enthusiasm for the bridge was high, and a bill was passed in 1930 to pay for the construction of the bridge.

How It Works Suspension bridges were built as far back as ancient times—in Europe, Asia, and Pre-Columbian America. The basic principle of a suspension bridge is that the footpath or roadway, called the deck, is suspended from ropes or chains. The ropes or chains are attached to supporting structures at either end of the span. Ancient suspension bridges were not rigid structures; they were made to sway in the wind. As early as the 7th century A.D., iron chains were first used as suspension lines in the Far East. These lines added stronger support for the deck. Design for modern suspension bridges evolved during the 19th and 20th centuries. Bridge spans became longer. One major innovation was the use of metal cables, composed of a bundle of wires, to support the weight of the deck. The Brooklyn Bridge, completed in 1883, was the first suspension span to use steel for its cable wires.

The special problems posed by building a bridge across the Golden Gate interested Joseph Strauss.

A Technical Masterpiece

Construction on the Golden Gate Bridge began in 1933. The bridge took four years to build and cost $35 million. Its 4,200-foot central span was the longest in the world until 1964. (In that year, New York City's Verrazano-Narrows Bridge surpassed it.)

Two support cables span the length of the Golden Gate Bridge. They carry the weight of the deck through a series of quadruple vertical cables running from each support cable to the deck. The cable lines are drawn tight by the tension created. The weight and tension created by all the cables is ultimately borne by enormous foundation towers at both ends of the bridge.

The entire bridge, including the approaches at either end, measures 8,981 feet in length. There are other remarkable features as well.

- The deck, which is 90 feet in width, accommodates six highway lanes.
- 80,000 miles of cable were used in the construction of the bridge.
- Each of the two support cables consists of 27,500 steel wires.
- Each of the two support cables weighs 24,500 tons.

The magnificent bridge was designed to span a bay of extraordinary width, and to withstand very strong currents and high winds.

Golden Gateway

On May 27, 1937—called Pedestrian Day—the bridge was opened. Approximately 200,000 people paid for the privilege of crossing the bridge that day. At noon the following day, President Franklin Delano Roosevelt touched a telegraph key in Washington. When that impulse reached San Francisco, cannons were fired and whistles sounded, and the bridge was officially opened to car traffic.

The Golden Gate Bridge helped San Francisco become a major city by linking it to the rest of prosperous northern California. The bridge also has become a symbol for San Francisco. It is admired as much for its beauty as it is for its technical achievement.

The designers and builders of the Golden Gate Bridge achieved a remarkable balance between technology and art. The impressive span, built to withstand the forces of nature, is both practical and in perfect harmony with its natural surroundings. The Golden Gate remains one of the most famous and most beautiful bridges in the world.

- The foundation towers, among the tallest bridge towers in the world, are 746 feet above the bay.

Solving the Problems One of the most difficult engineering problems was building the foundations for the towers. These were laid on bedrock 100 feet below the water's surface. But strong tidal currents made the completion of this task extremely hazardous for the workers. First, they had to build a cofferdam, which is a watertight case kept dry by pumps. Within these huge chambers, workers could build the foundations. However, with the diving equipment available at that time, divers could work for only four 20-minute periods each day to build the cofferdam.

The engineers also had to take into account the natural reactions to changing temperatures of the concrete, cable wires, and other materials, which expand in the heat and shrink in the cold. They designed the towers and cables to adjust for these changes. Thus, the midpoint of the bridge can sink up to five feet below its normal level in cold weather and rise up to six feet in hot weather. Strauss also calculated for the high wind-driven waves in the bay and allowed a 220-foot clearance at high water for ships.

Unforeseen Events The construction of this magnificent bridge was not without tragedy. Eleven workers were killed during the construction. In another unfortunate incident, a ship lost its bearings in a heavy fog and hit the south tower. The south tower was damaged a second time before its completion, that time by a storm.

This table lists some of the major suspension bridges around the world.

MAJOR SUSPENSION BRIDGES			
Bridge	**Location**	**Main Span (feet)**	**Date Completed**
Humber	Humber River, Hull, England	4,626	1981
Verrazano-Narrows	New York Harbor, N.Y.	4,260	1964
Golden Gate	San Francisco Bay, California	4,200	1937
Mackinac Straits	Straits of Mackinac, Michigan	3,800	1957
Bosporus	Bosporus Strait, Istanbul, Turkey	3,524	1973
George Washington	Hudson River, Fort Lee, N.J., to New York, N.Y.	3,500	1931
Ponte 25 de Abril	Tagus River, Lisbon, Portugal	3,323	1966
New Forth Road	Firth of Forth, Queensferry, Scotland	3,300	1964
Pierre Laporte	St. Lawrence River, Quebec, Canada	2,190	1970
Brooklyn	East River, New York, N.Y.	1,595	1883

The Sears Tower

Completed in 1974, this Chicago skyscraper became the tallest building in the world.

The Skyscraper Age

America's cities were growing rapidly in the late 1800s. Buildings were becoming larger to accommodate the increasing population. However, traditional buildings were limited in their height because they required thick walls to support their bulk. The development of iron and steel girders capable of supporting the weight of many floors made skyscrapers possible. Secured in a concrete foundation, these metal frames were strong, but lightweight. Architects were now able to design taller structures. This ability became especially important in large cities where land was increasingly scarce and expensive. Thus, cities like Chicago and New York began to build upward instead of outward.

Rise of the Skyscraper Chicago, destroyed by fire in 1871, became the center of modern construction. The fire gave architects an opportunity to test new construction ideas as they rebuilt the city. The first steel-framed skyscraper—the ten-story Home Insurance Company Building, designed by William Jenney—was completed in that city in 1884.

The first New York City skyscraper was built on a site only 21 feet wide. Designed by Bradford Gilbert, the 13-story Tower Building on lower Broadway was completed in 1888. By the early 20th century, New York had become the skyscraper capital.

At the time of its completion in 1931, New York City's Empire State Building was the tallest building in the world. Its height of 102 stories includes the observation tower on its roof. In 1973, the World Trade Center, known as New York's "twin towers," became the world's tallest skyscrapers. This honor lasted only one year. In 1974, the city of Chicago once again claimed to be the home of the world's tallest building.

Sears, Roebuck and Company

One of the oldest retail firms in the United States—Sears, Roebuck and Company—decided to expand its business. As part of the expansion, the company planned to build new corporate headquarters on a two-block site in downtown Chicago. In an unusual construction strategy, the company planned the structure from the inside out. Planners determined the location and size of every department. They even projected office requirements to the year 2003. Then they hired an architectural firm to design a building to accommodate this interior plan. Sears executives selected the Chicago firm of Skidmore, Owings, and Merrill (known as SOM) to design the structure. SOM was well known for its skyscrapers, which include Lever House in New York City and the John Hancock Center in Chicago. SOM's skyscrapers were designed for function, with little decoration and large areas of glass. This "glass box" design had become the standard style for high-rise buildings during the 1950s and 1960s.

COMPARING SKYSCRAPERS				
Building	City	Stories	Height (feet)	Year Completed
Sears Tower	Chicago	110	1,454	1974
World Trade Center	New York	110	1,350	1973
Empire State Building	New York	102	1,250	1931
John Hancock Center	Chicago	100	1,127	1970
Central Plaza	Hong Kong	78	1,028	1992
First Interstate World Center	Los Angeles	73	1,018	1989
Bank of Montreal Tower (First Canadian Place Building)	Toronto	73	935	1973
Messe Twin Building	Frankfurt	70	841	1990
Scotia Plaza	Toronto	68	906	1988
C & S Plaza	Atlanta	57	1,050	1992

This table compares some of the tallest buildings in the world. Except for the Empire State Building, they were all completed after 1970.

Unlike other skyscrapers, the Sears Tower was designed from the inside out. It is actually nine separate towers that, when joined, support the entire structure.

Building a Tower

From the Inside Out Departing from the single-towered glass box, SOM created a new design for the Sears building. Based on the interior specifications Sears had provided, SOM proposed a structure that would consist of nine square "tubes" of varying heights. Each of these actually would be an individual building. The joined tubes would work together to support the entire structure. This arrangement also would mean that the building would need less steel than is usually required for a skyscraper.

Concrete, Steel, and Glass Workers excavated a huge trench and filled it with concrete for the foundation. This enormous slab keeps the building from sinking into the ground. Then, giant steel "legs" were secured in the foundation. Next, welded steel frames formed the vertical tubes to provide the rigid skeleton needed to limit the sway of the building in the strong Chicago winds. Workers used prefabricated steel for the frame, and most of the welding was done off-site. Ironworkers standing on steel beams high above the street put the final bolts into place.

The exterior of the building is black aluminum and bronze-tinted glass. Black bands circle the building between floors 30 and 31, 48 and 49, 64 and 65, and 106 and 108. The bands conceal areas of the building that house air-conditioning and heating units and other building maintenance equipment.

About 60 percent of the building's bulk is contained in the first 50 floors. Two of the nine tubes—at opposite sides of the building—end at the 50th floor. Two more tubes end at the 66th floor; three end at the 89th floor. The remaining two towers rise another 20 stories.

Dominating the Chicago skyline, the Sears Tower has become one of the city's most important landmarks.

Chicago Landmark

The Sears Tower—110 stories and 1,454 feet high—cost $150 million to build. It contains 80 miles of elevator cable and enough concrete to cover 78 football fields. Six thousand homes could be cooled by the tower's huge air-conditioning system.

When the tower was completed in 1974, it surpassed the World Trade Center as the tallest building in the world. Sears, Roebuck and Company occupied the first 50 floors, where the huge interior space did indeed fit the company's needs. The upper floors were leased to other companies.

The Sears Tower had its critics. Some Chicagoans believed that it would increase traffic congestion in the Loop, Chicago's downtown area. Others disliked its unconventional appearance. It does not have the sleek glass walls of other skyscrapers. The tubes ending at several different levels give the structure a jagged appearance. Over the years, however, the criticism has given way to acceptance, and the Sears Tower has become a famous Chicago landmark dominating the city's skyline.

English Channel Tunnel

Opened in 1994, the world's longest underwater tunnel links England and France for the first time in 8,000 years.

The English Channel

The English Channel is the body of water that lies between England and France and connects the Atlantic Ocean and the North Sea. Scientists believe that the channel was formed during the Ice Age, about 8,000 years ago. Melting ice flooded a low plain or isthmus that once joined England and France.

The English Channel is about 350 miles long. It ranges in width from 21 to 100 miles. The narrowest part of the channel is called the Strait of Dover. It lies between Dover, England, and Calais, France. With nearly 600 vessels going through or across the Dover Strait daily, it is the world's busiest sea passage. Rough seas and strong currents, frequent bad weather, and dense fogs make it a dangerous route. The idea of a safer and faster link between England and the European mainland has existed since the 18th century.

The first proposal to build a tunnel under the English Channel was made by French geologist Nicholas Desmaret in 1751. Nobody thought it practical, and the idea was dropped. Fifty years later, French mining engineer Albert Mathieu presented another plan. This one had the support of Napoleon Bonaparte but not the British, who continued to reject such proposals on the grounds of national security.

By the 1950s, Great Britain had warmed to the idea of a channel tunnel—a railway link between the two countries. Britain and France formed the Anglo-French Channel Tunnel Study Group to carry out a series of surveys and studies. Then, in 1973, the British Parliament approved the channel tunnel project. In a formal agreement signed by British prime minister Margaret Thatcher and French president François Mitterrand in 1986, the two nations agreed to certain terms. The tunnel would be privately funded through bank loans and stock sales. At a cost of more than $12 billion, the Channel Tunnel is the most ambitious engineering project ever undertaken in Europe. Eurotunnel—a new British and French company—was established to own and operate the tunnel.

Because the Channel Tunnel is one of the largest engineering projects in history, no single construction company could handle it alone. A partnership of ten major engineering firms—five British and five French—was formed to design and build the tunnel. This construction company is called Transmanche-Link.

The Channel Tunnel—or Chunnel, as it is sometimes called—is actually three tunnels. Two tunnels carry passengers and freight by rail. A service tunnel between the rail tunnels is used for maintenance and emergencies.

A tunnel boring machine is about 30 feet high and as long as two football fields. It is capable of digging nearly 350 yards a week.

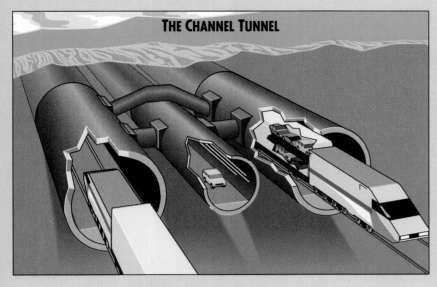

THE CHANNEL TUNNEL

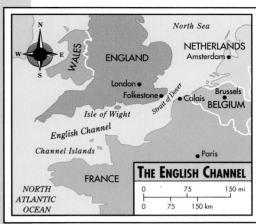

THE ENGLISH CHANNEL

The Channel Tunnel *(left)* actually is three separate tunnels—two for trains going in each direction and one for service vehicles. The tunnel is located between Calais and Folkestone as shown on this map.

Boring a Tunnel

Actual work on the Chunnel began in 1987. Workers built deep shafts at Calais in France and at Folkestone in England. Huge tunnel-boring machines, or TBMs, were lowered into the shafts in sections, then assembled at tunnel level. Six TBMs—three on each side—began boring huge underwater passageways toward each other below the channel. The TBMs, guided by lasers, were so accurate that, when the first two sections of tunnel met in 1990, they were off by only 20 inches.

Construction Challenges

Each TBM was equipped with machinery and conveyor belts to lift and carry away the debris. Concrete tunnel sections were put in place and cemented together. Some sections have prefabricated cast-iron linings for additional strength.

Crossover passageways from the rail tunnels to the service tunnel were constructed every 1,200 feet. Specially designed multipurpose vehicles, capable of running in both directions, are used to make emergency repairs and for evacuation, if necessary.

Workers installed ducts, called air spades, every 650 feet along the rail tunnels. As the trains barrel through the tunnels, they push air before them at hurricane force (about 75 miles per hour). By creating a place for it to go, the air spades relieve that air pressure.

Working conditions were difficult and dangerous. Those on the French side had to dig through harder rock on that coast. In addition, workers had to cope with fumes, chalk dust, and the incredibly loud noise of the TBMs. Five workers died, one of whom was crushed by a truck removing debris.

Building delays and a lack of funds plagued the project along the way. In 1991, the construction group faced an unforeseen problem. The length, depth, and narrow width of the rail tunnels, combined with heat created by the high-speed trains, would result in 130-degree temperatures in the tunnels. The builders needed to find a way to keep the tunnels cool. The problem was solved by building huge coolers on each side of the crossing. Cold water is pumped from the coolers through pipes running the length of each tunnel.

High-speed Links

The two rail tunnels were completed in the spring of 1991. All that remained was the installation of the air-conditioning, power, and signal systems. After several postponements, the Chunnel finally opened in 1994. High-speed electric trains carry passengers and cars at about 100 miles per hour. The trip under the English Channel takes about 30 to 35 minutes. (A ferry trip takes about one and one-half hours.)

New highways to connect London and Paris to the Chunnel are in the planning stages. The combined superhighways and rail tunnels will make the journey from London to Paris in about four hours.

The Chunnel is changing travel and trade between Europe and Great Britain. The French are more enthusiastic about these changes than the British. The French expect business to boom in areas near the Chunnel entrance as well as along the connecting roads. Many British people, however, see the changes as a disruption of their traditional way of life.

Glossary

Acropolis: The sacred place at the top of a hill in central Athens. It was the site of an ancient fortress and contained several important structures, including the Parthenon.

adobe: Brick made of mud mixed with straw or reeds that is dried in the sun; a building made of adobe bricks.

amphitheater: A building with seats that rise in curved rows around an open space in which games or plays take place.

arsenal: A place for manufacturing and storing weapons.

Athena: The Greek goddess of wisdom and the protector of Athens.

baray: One of the reservoirs built in Cambodia during the time of the ancient Khmer Empire. They were used to store water from monsoons and snow runoff.

bas-relief: A sculpture in which a design is raised slightly from its background.

Beefeater: A Yeoman Warder, or guard, of the Tower of London. They once guarded the tower complex, but today they have mostly ceremonial duties and serve as tourist guides.

Bronze Age: The period in human history from about 3500 B.C. to 1000 B.C., characterized by the use of bronze tools and weapons.

cathedral: A church that is the official seat of a bishop; also, a large, important church.

Classical Age: Refers to the ancient Greek and Roman civilizations, especially to developments in art, literature, architecture, and philosophy.

coat of arms: A group of emblems and figures arranged on a shield that serve as a special identifying insignia for a person, a family, an institution, or a country.

cofferdam: A watertight case, kept dry by pumps, that enables workers to construct underwater foundations.

cupola: A small, domelike structure on the roof of a building.

exposition: A public exhibit of artistic or industrial developments.

frieze: A sculptured or richly ornamented band, as around a building.

gladiator: In ancient Rome, a man who fought to the death for public entertainment. Slaves, criminals, and prisoners of war were trained to be gladiators.

glyph: A pictograph or other symbolic sign or character, especially when carved into a surface.

Golden Age: Refers to the period in Greek history from about 477 B.C. to 431 B.C. when some of Greece's most important achievements took place. The term also may refer to a flourishing and prosperous period in any civilization.

Gothic: A style of architecture that was widespread in Europe in the late 12th through the early 16th century. Following the Romanesque period, Gothic architecture featured lightness and immense size, pointed arches and spires, vaulting, and decorative elements such as sculptures and stained glass windows.

hieroglyphics: Ancient form of writing in which sounds, syllables, and words are represented by pictures instead of by alphabetic letters. The Egyptians and the Mayans are two cultures that used hieroglyphics.

hydroelectric power: Electricity produced by converting the energy of running water.

Iron Age: Period in human history from about 1000 B.C. to A.D. 100 characterized by the introduction and development of iron tools and weapons. The Iron Age followed the Bronze Age.

keep: The strongest and most secure part of a castle or fort, usually located in the center.

kiva: A ceremonial room found in many Pueblo Indian cliff dwellings, usually round and partly underground.

Koran: The sacred book of the Islamic religion, which contains its religious teachings and moral codes.

levee: A dike or embankment, usually along a river, created to prevent flooding.

limestone: Rock that is formed by the remains of shells and coral. It consists mainly of calcium carbonate and is used for building.

mastaba: In ancient Egypt, a flat-topped stone structure used for burial.

mesa: A flat-topped hill or a small plateau with steep sides.

minaret: A tall, slender tower on a mosque, which has a balcony from which Muslims are called to prayer.

mirador: A small enclosure, such as a turret or a balcony, with several arched openings.

moat: A deep, wide trench around the walls of a fortress or a castle that usually is filled with water and is used for protection.

mosaic: A design made by fitting together pieces of stone, glass, or tile of different colors and cementing them into place.

mosque: A Muslim place of worship.

motte and bailey: An early type of castle fortification in which an enclosed wooden structure was situated on a mound surrounded by a ditch.

mummy: A body wrapped in cloth and specially treated to preserve it.

nave: The long central main section of a church interior.

nomadic tribe: A group of people with no permanent home, who move about constantly in search of food and pasturelands.

Pax Romana: The approximately 200 years of peace in Roman history that followed the founding of the Roman Empire by Augustus in 27 B.C.

pediment: In Classical Greek architecture, an ornamental triangular piece, usually over a doorway or a fireplace.

pilaster: A decorative column partly built into a wall and partly projecting from it.

polder: An area of lowland that is reclaimed from a body of water. A polder is created by the construction of a dike.

prefabricate: To design and manufacture parts at a factory and transport these parts to a construction site for assembling.

pumice: Spongy, light, and porous volcanic rock formed from rapidly cooling lava.

quarry: An open pit for obtaining some types of building materials, such as slate or limestone.

Romanesque: A style of architecture of the Middle Ages that is characterized by rounded arches, thick walls, few small windows, sparse decoration, and solid, heavy-looking structures.

Rosetta stone: A black stone tablet that contains inscriptions in Greek and in Egyptian hieroglyphics and in the characters used by the general population of Egypt. The Rosetta stone provided the key to deciphering ancient Egyptian writings.

sarcophagus: A stone coffin that is raised above ground level.

Silk Road: A trading route across the desert west of China, named for the silk that the Chinese traded.

stained glass: Pieces of colored glass that are joined to create designs, such as those in church windows.

stalactite: A deposit of calcium carbonate that hangs from the roof of a cavern like an icicle. Stalactites can also be handmade—lacy, icicle-shaped forms carved in plaster or stone.

stucco: A plaster cement used to cover an exterior wall or to decorate an interior wall.

suspension bridge: A bridge that has its roadway suspended from cables or chains that are strung from towers and strongly anchored at the ends.

TBM: A tunnel boring machine such as those used to build the English Channel Tunnel.

terpen: Great mounds of earth and clay, built on wet and marshy land, on which people constructed their homes. Early settlements in the Netherlands often were built on terpens.

thatch: Plant material, such as reeds, grass clippings, or straw, that is used as a roof or cover.

wrought iron: A commercial form of iron that is relatively soft but tough and can be hammered and shaped.

Suggested Readings

Note: An asterisk (*) denotes a Young Adult title.

*Baudez, Claude, and Picasso, Sydney. *Lost Cities of the Maya.* Abrams, 1992.

Blunden, Carolyn, and Elvin, Mark. *Cultural Atlas of China.* Facts on File, 1983.

*Chandler, David P. *The Land and People of Cambodia.* HarperCollins, 1991.

Cornell, Tim, and Matthews, John. *Atlas of the Roman World.* Facts on File, 1982.

Fry, Somerset. *The Tower of London.* Hippocrene Books, 1991.

Garlake, Peter. *The Kingdoms of Africa: The Making of the Past.* Peter Bedrick Books, 1991.

Goldberger, Paul. *The Skyscraper.* Knopf, 1983.

*Haberman, Arthur, and Hundey, Ian. *Civilizations: A Cultural Atlas.* Gage, 1994.

Hawkes, Nigel. *Structures: The Way Things Are Built.* Macmillan, 1993.

Jackson, Donald. *Great American Bridges and Dams.* Preservation Press, 1988.

*Macauley, David. *Cathedral.* Houghton Mifflin, 1981.

*————. *Pyramid.* Houghton Mifflin, 1975.

*————. *The Way Things Work.* Houghton Mifflin, 1988.

Mallows, Wilfrid. *The Mystery of Great Zimbabwe.* Norton, 1984.

*Mason, Antony. *Southeast Asia.* Raintree Steck-Vaughn, 1992.

*McDonald, Fiona, and Bergin, Mark. *A Greek Temple.* Peter Bedrick Books, 1992.

*McDonald, Fiona, and James, John. *A Medieval Cathedral.* Peter Bedrick Books, 1991.

*Milner, Cate. *France.* Raintree Steck-Vaughn, 1990.

*Morley, Jacqueline; Bergin, Mark; and James, John. *An Egyptian Pyramid.* Peter Bedrick Books, 1991.

*Morrison, Ian A. *Egypt.* Raintree Steck-Vaughn, 1991.

Murray, Jocelyn. *Cultural Atlas of Africa.* Facts on File, 1981.

*Perdrizet, Marie-Pierre. *The Cathedral Builders.* Millbrook Press, 1992.

*Poulton, Michael. *Life in the Time of Augustus and the Ancient Romans.* Raintree Steck-Vaughn, 1993.

**Rand McNally Children's Atlas of Native Americans.* Rand McNally, 1992.

**Rand McNally Children's Atlas of World History.* Rand McNally, 1991.

Sabloff, Jeremy A. *The Cities of Ancient Mexico: Reconstructing a Lost World.* Thames & Hudson, 1989.

Schwatz, Daniel. *The Great Wall of China.* Thames & Hudson, 1990.

*Spangenburg, Ray, and Moser, Diane K. *The Story of America's Bridges.* Facts on File, 1991.

Stevens, Joseph E. *Hoover Dam: An American Adventure.* University of Oklahoma Press, 1990.

*Trout, Lawana Hooper. *The Maya.* Chelsea House, 1991.

**Visual Dictionary of Buildings.* Dorling Kindersley, 1992.

*Waterlow, Julia. *Nile.* Raintree Steck-Vaughn, 1993.

Wilson, Derek. *Breakthrough: Tunneling the Channel.* Trafalgar Books, 1991.

Index